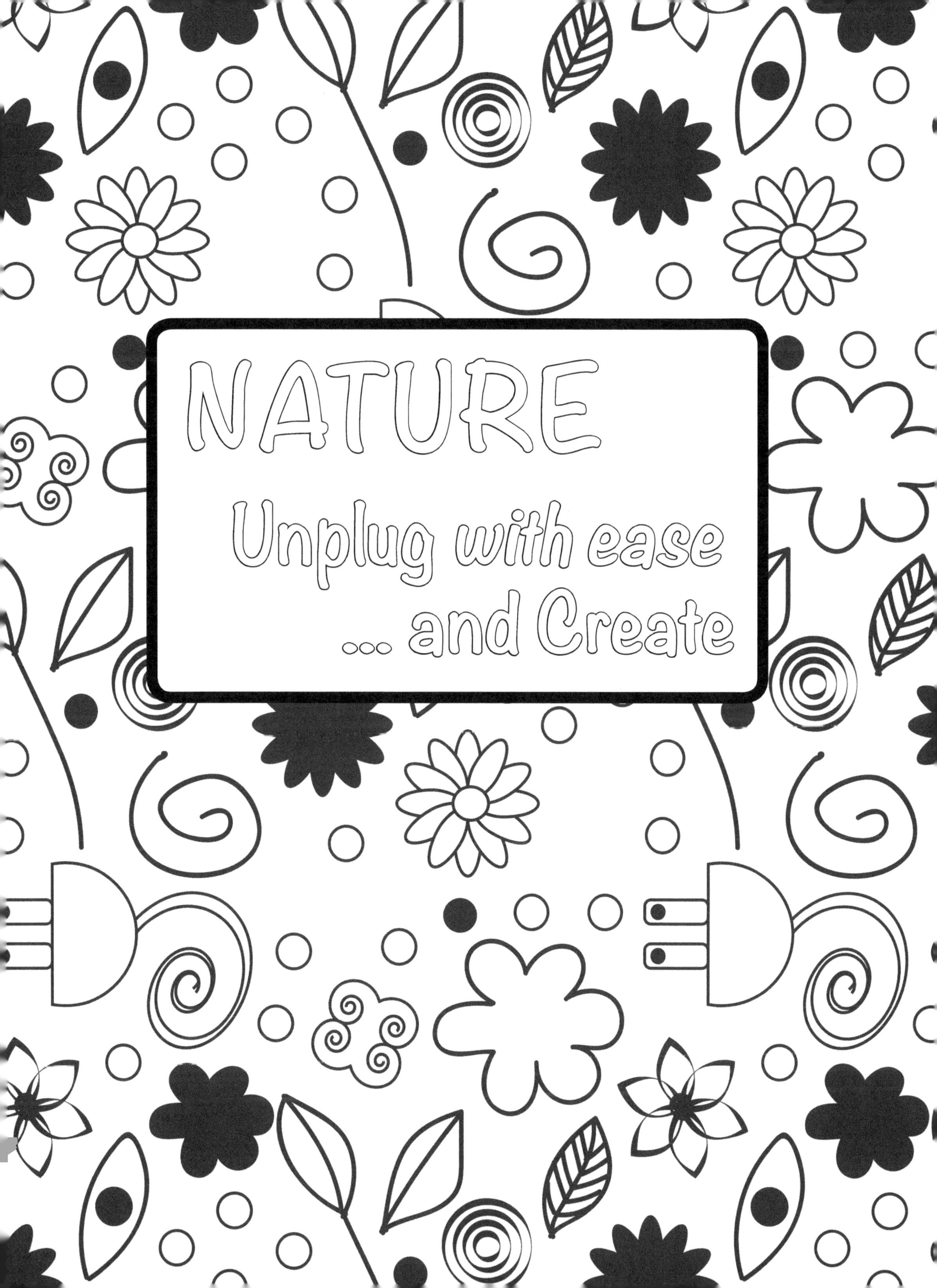
NATURE
Unplug with ease
... and Create

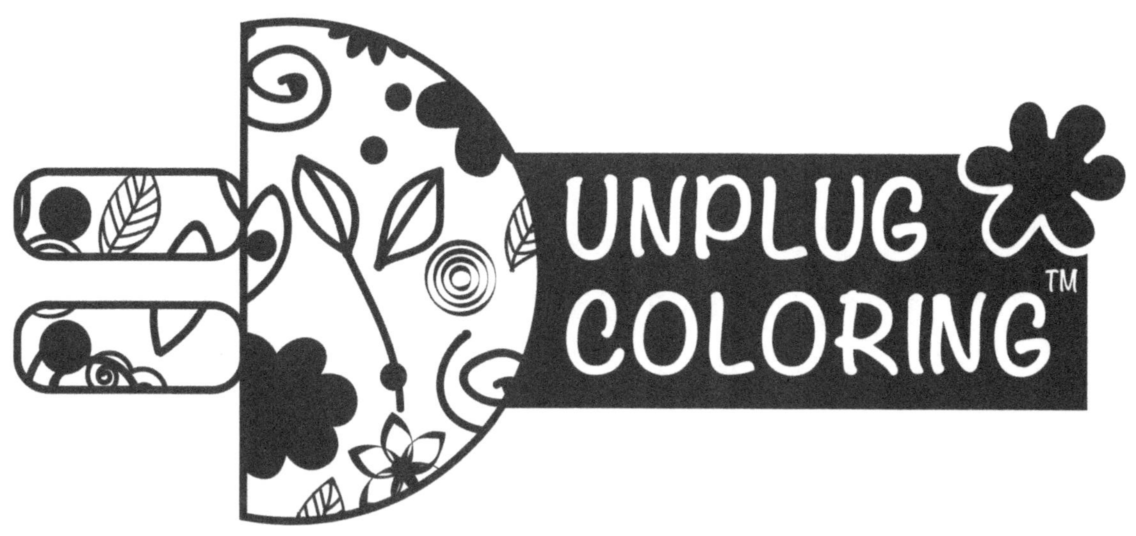

Visit unplugcoloring.com

for free coloring sheets and keep

CONNECTED

to us!

Published by Unplug Coloring
Fishers, IN 46037
www.unplugcoloring.com
sales@unplugcoloring.com

Design and production: Unplug Coloring

ISBN: 978-0-9974900-1-5

Made in the USA

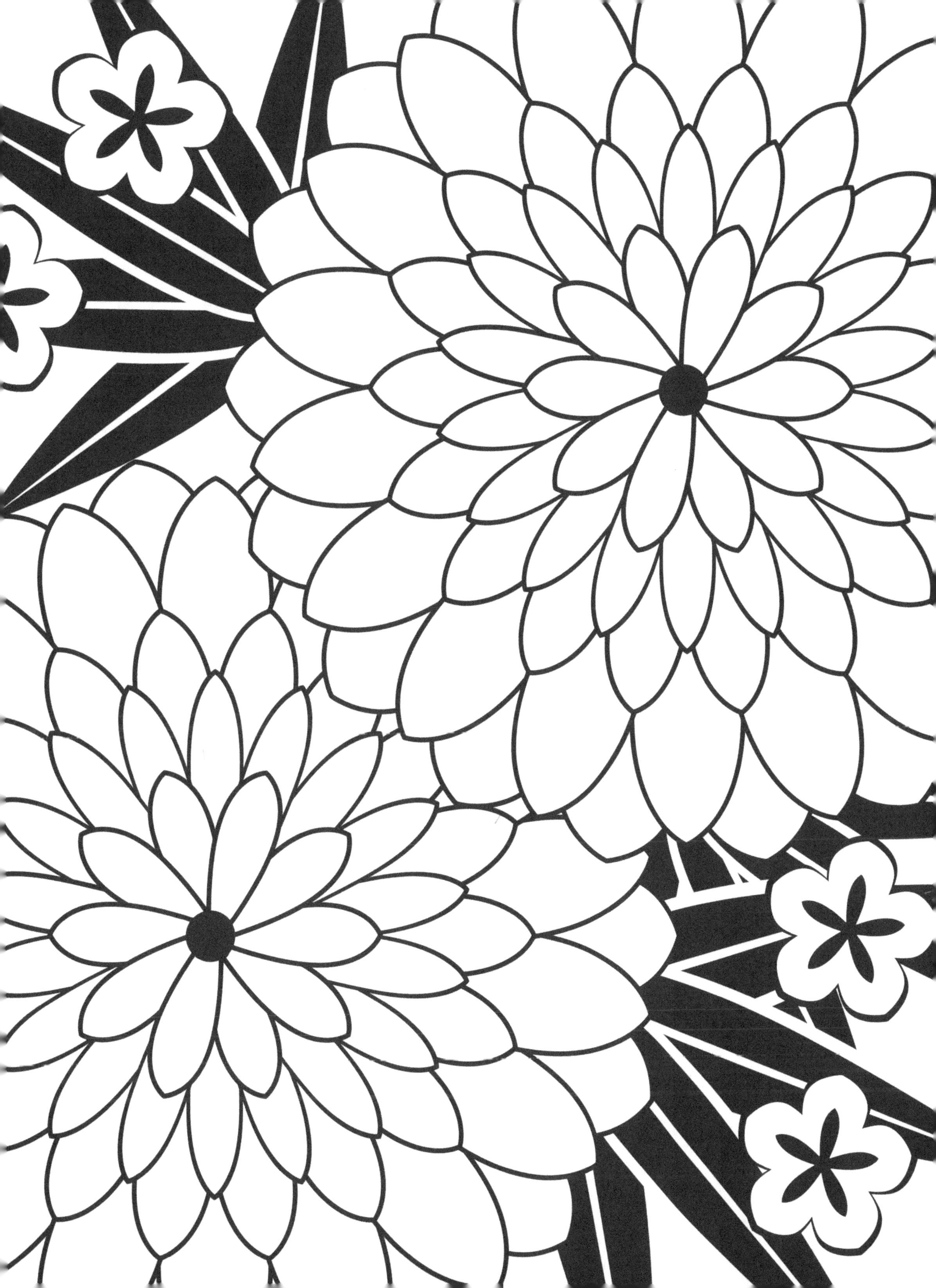

Blotter

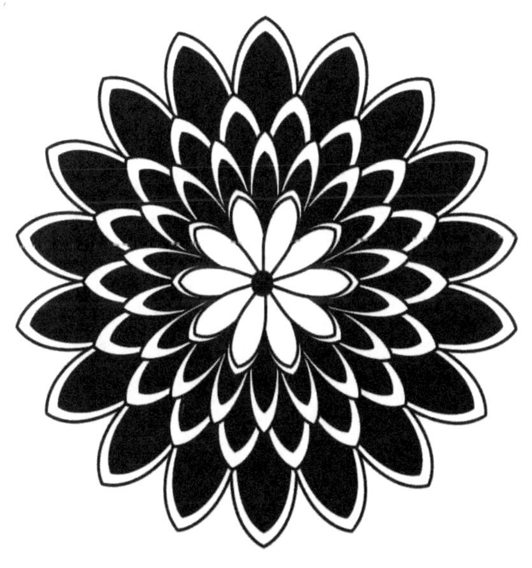

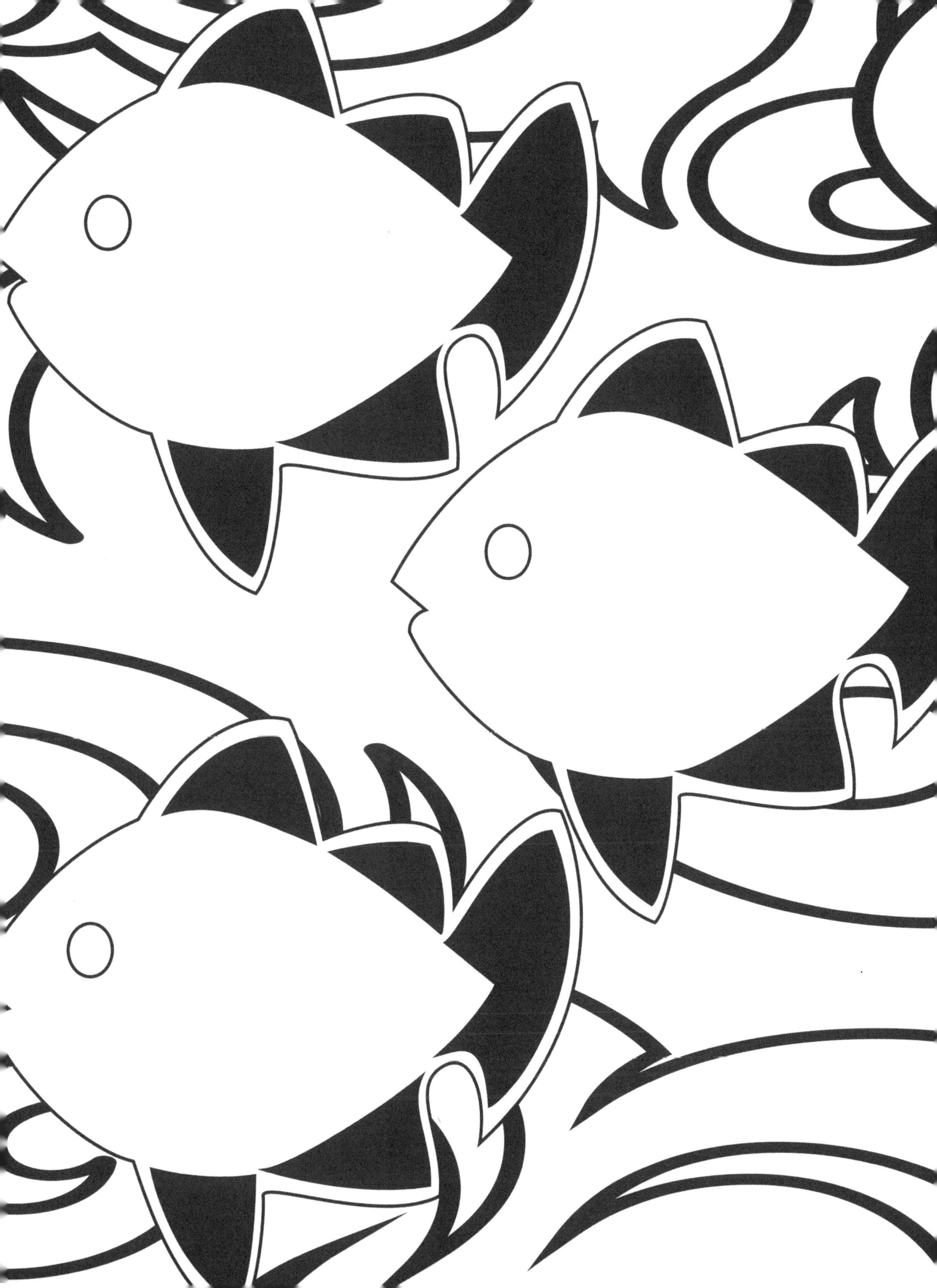

Blotter

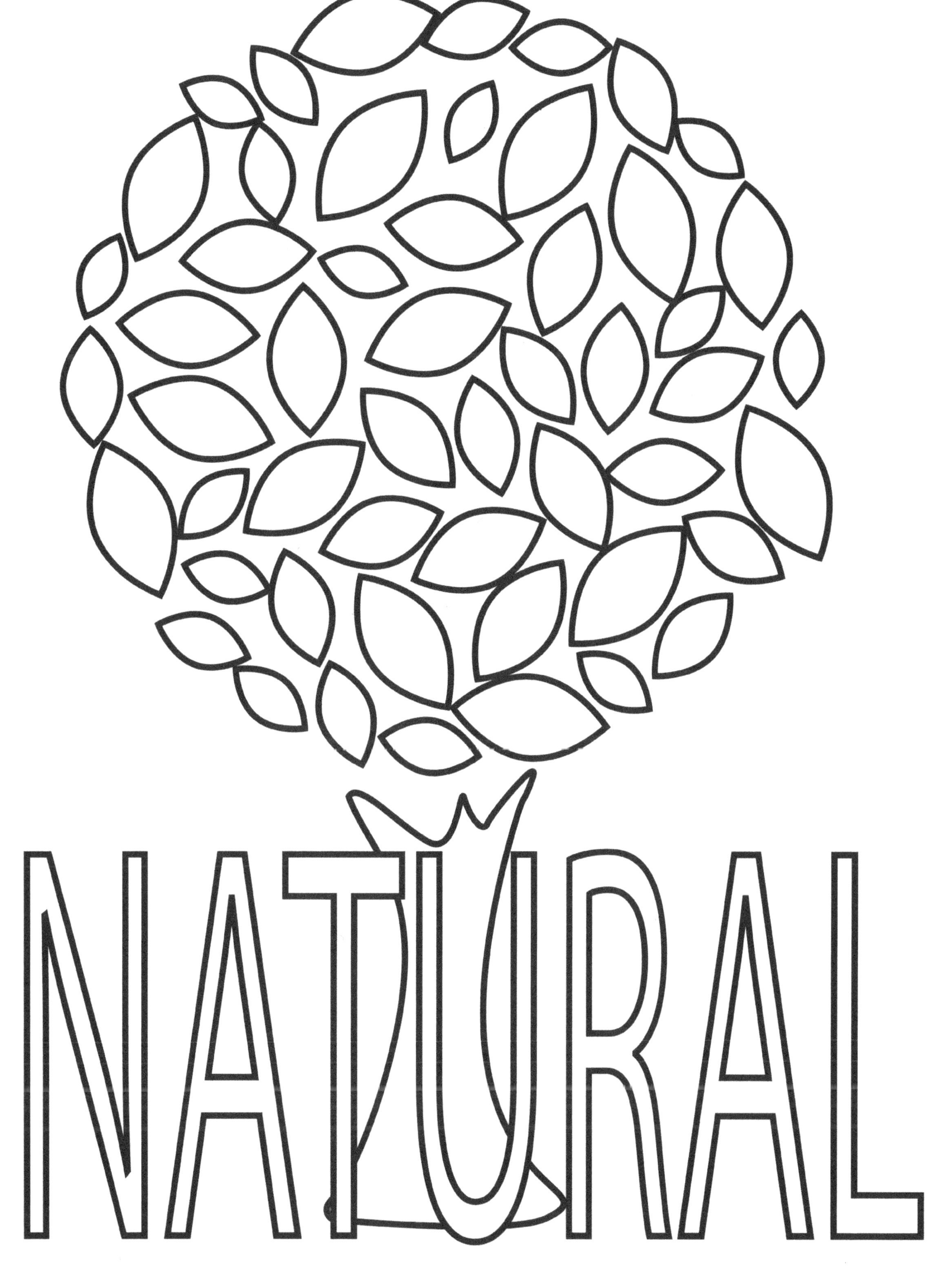
NATURAL

Blotter

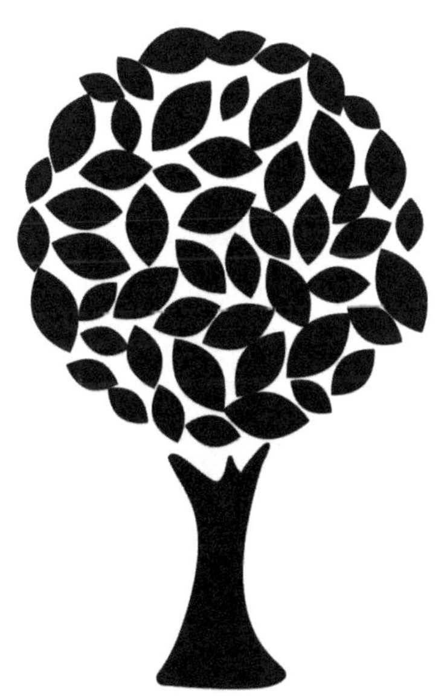

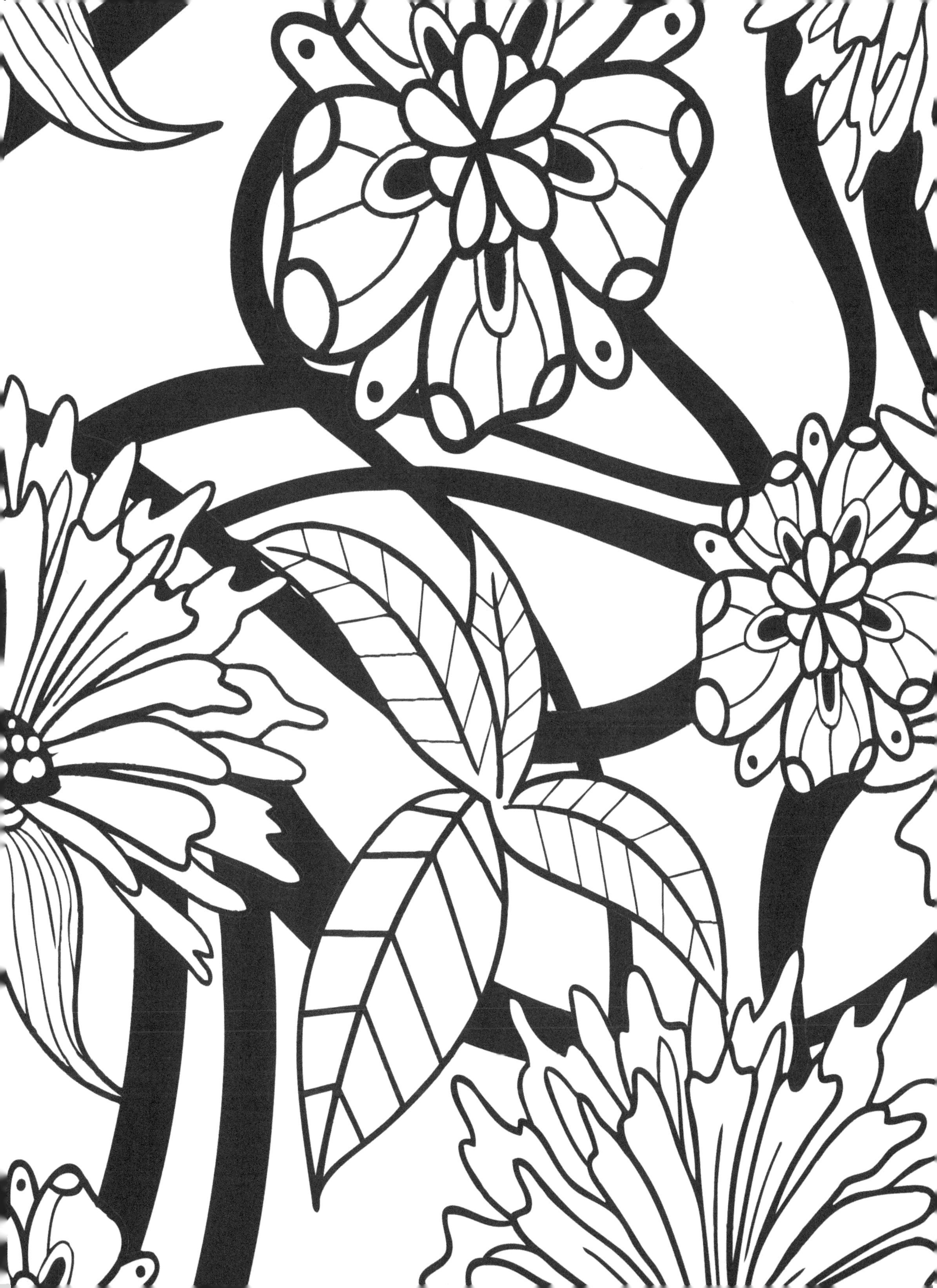

Blotter

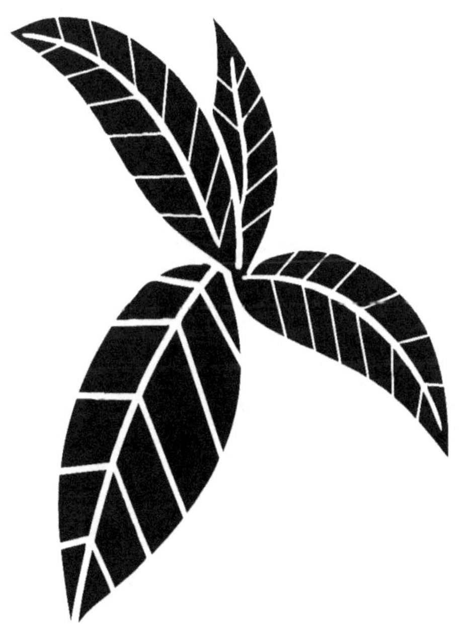

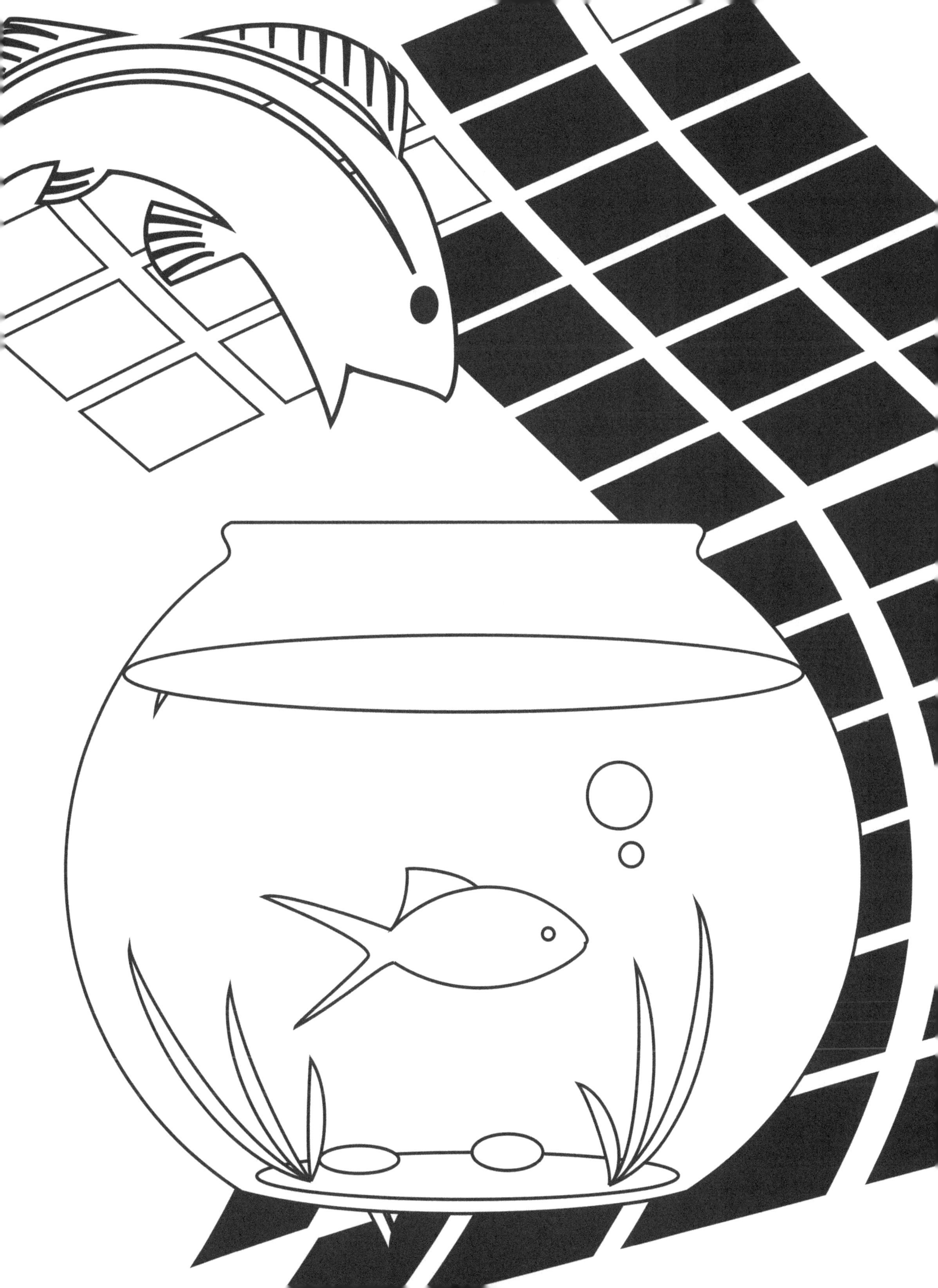

Blotter

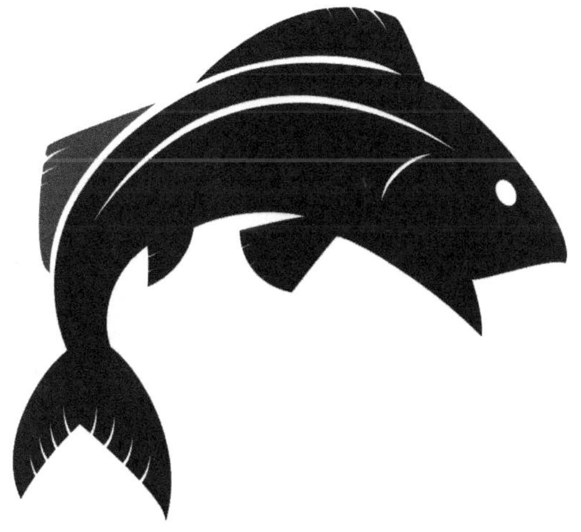

Blotter

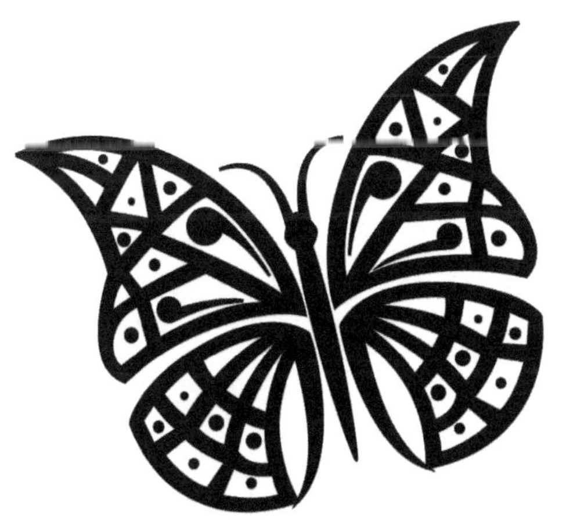

Blotter

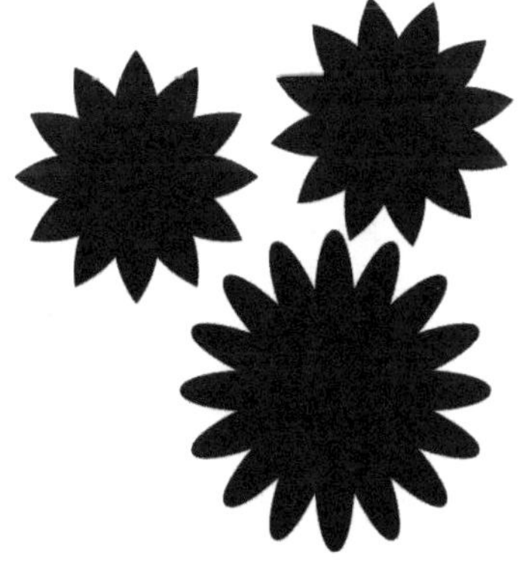

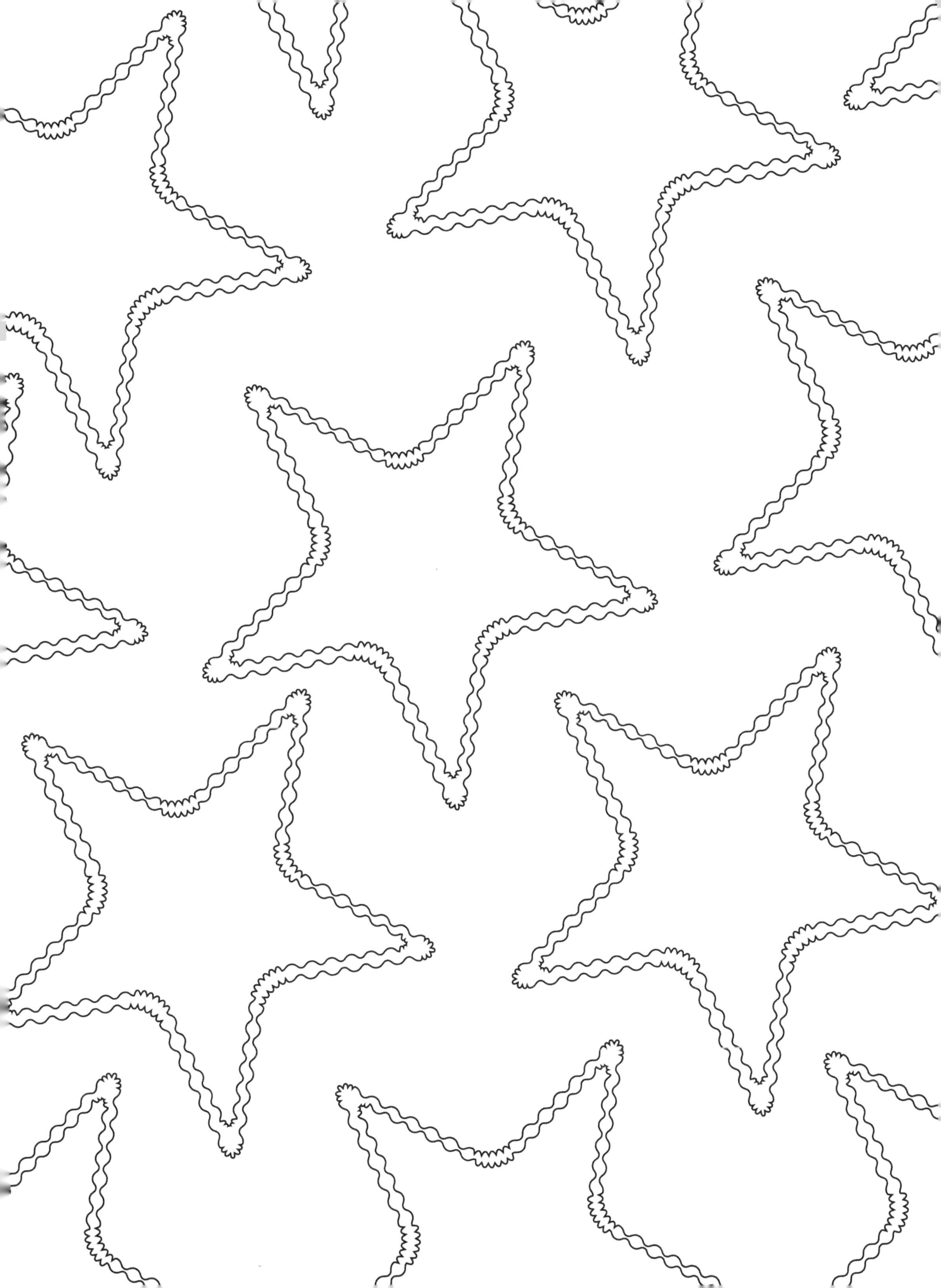

Blotter

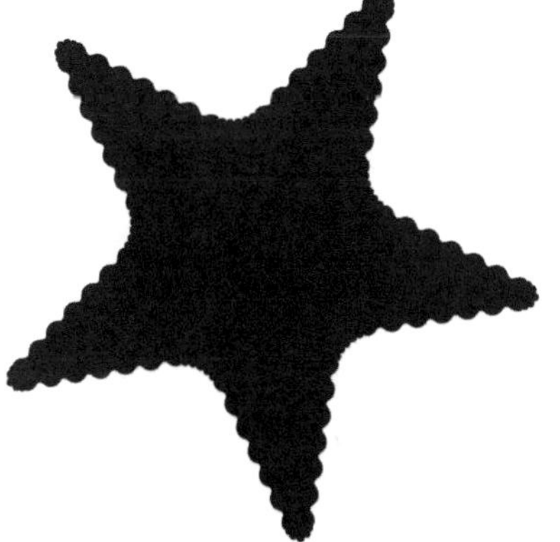

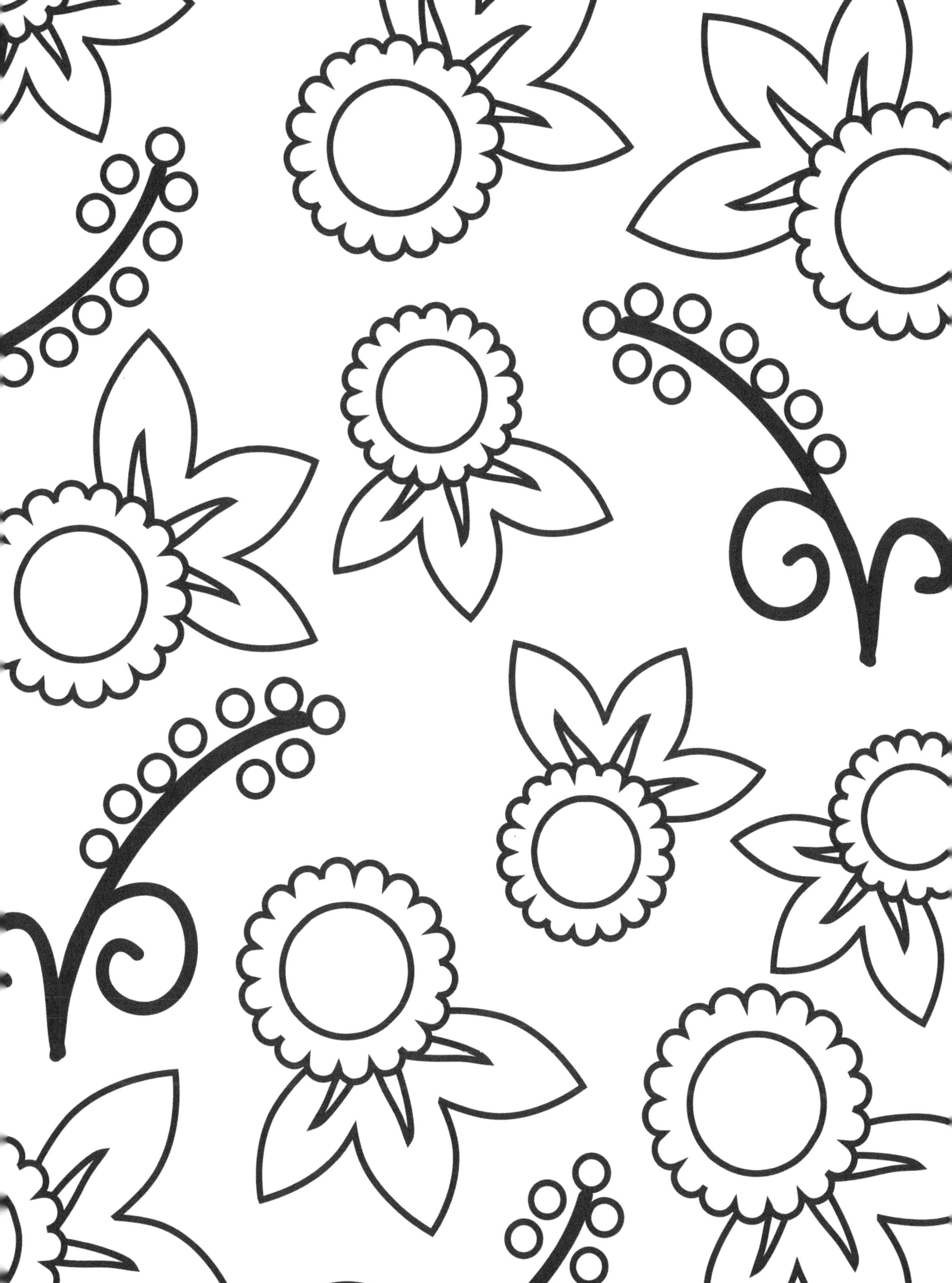

Blotter

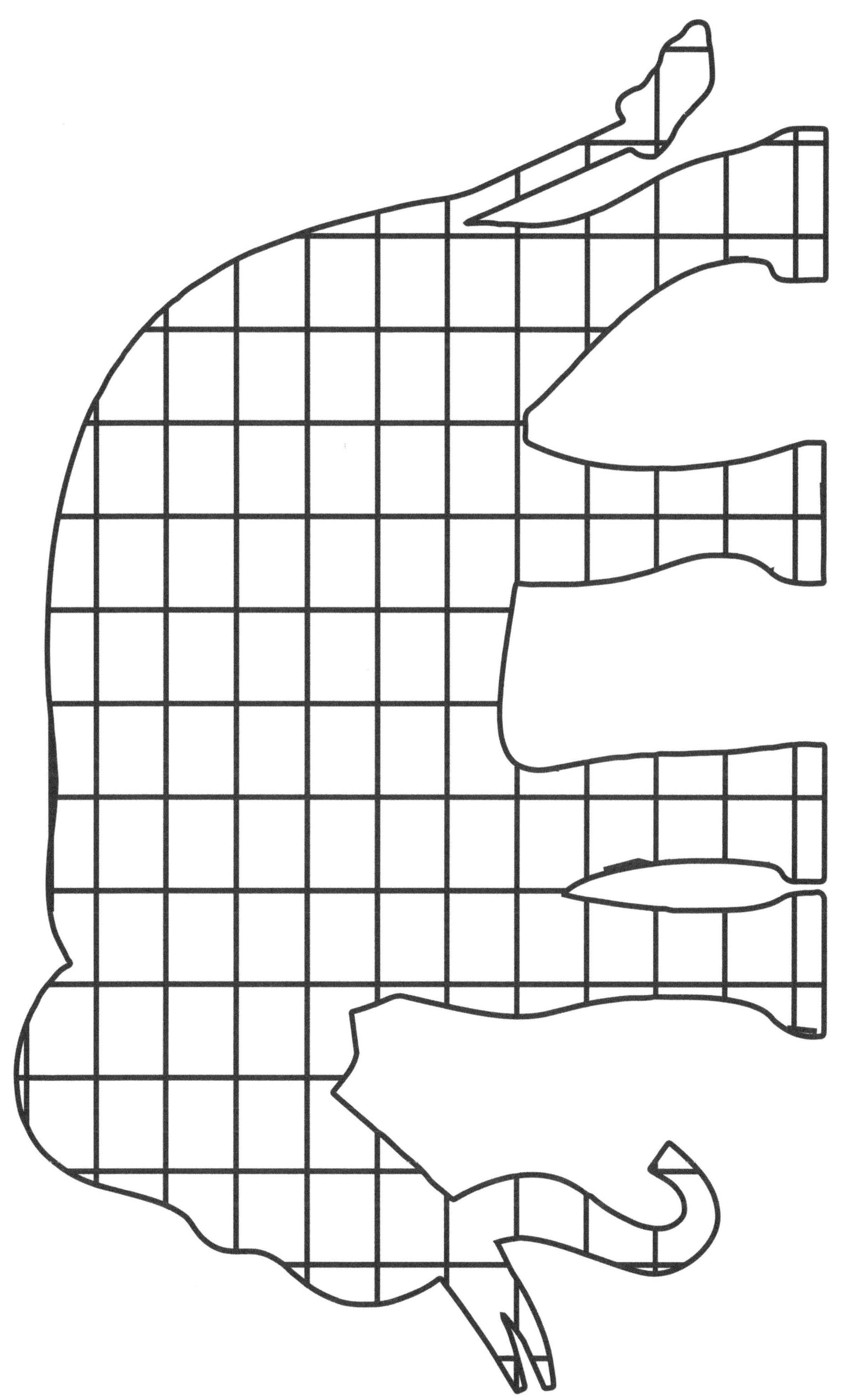

Blotter

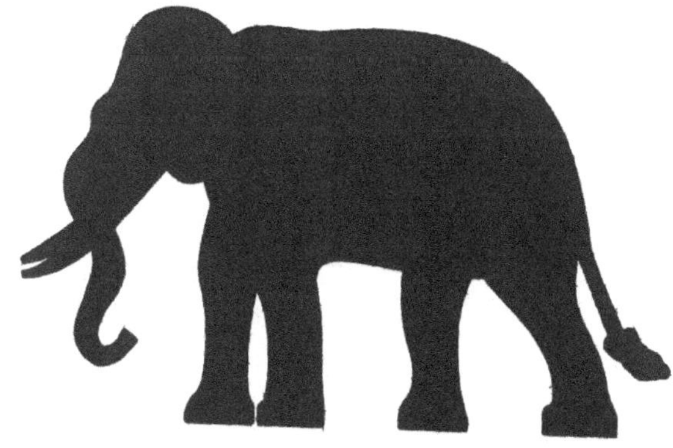

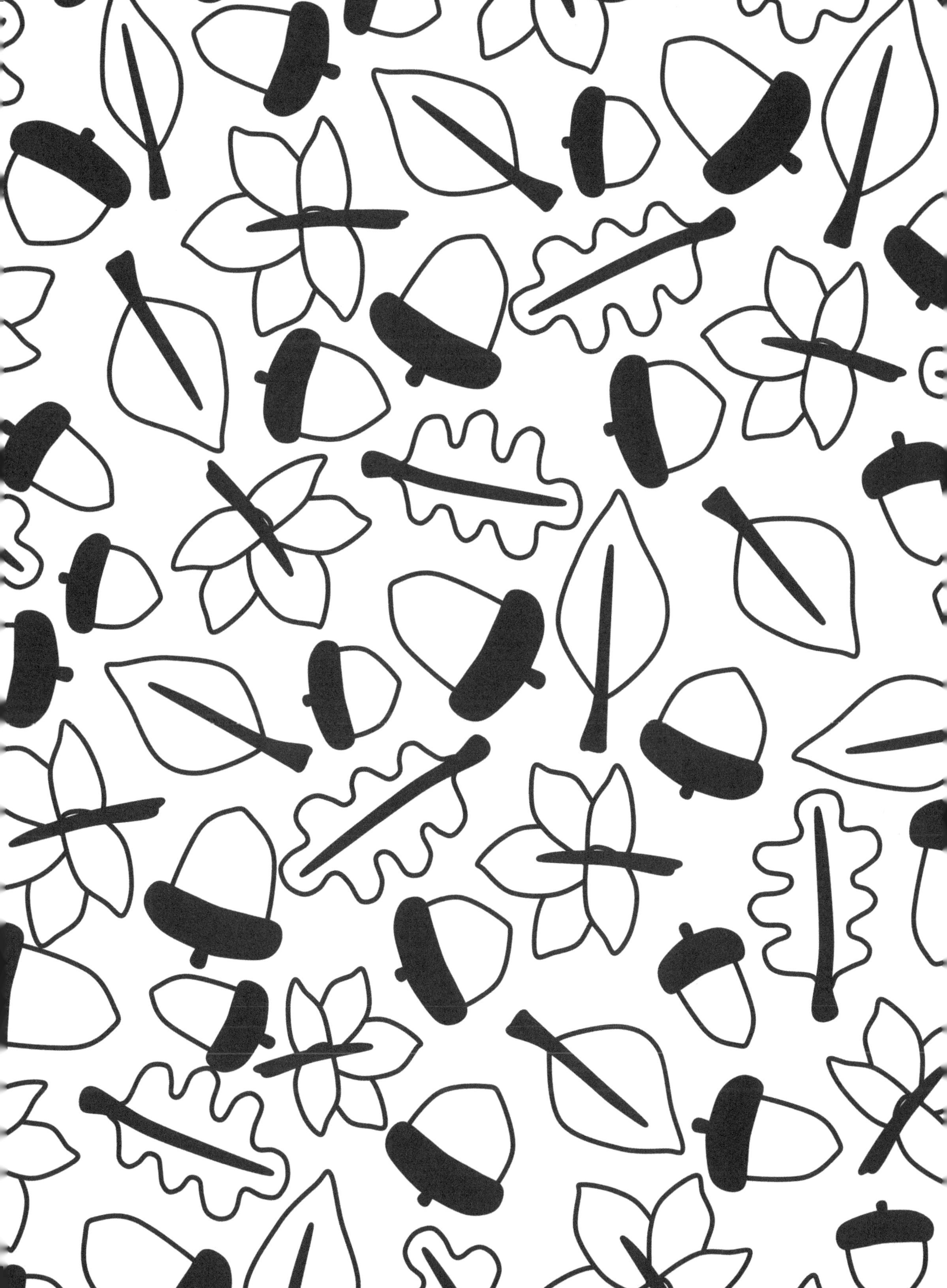

Blotter

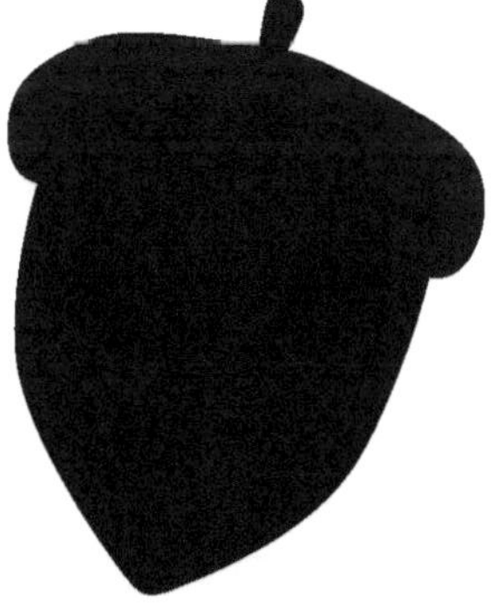

Blotter

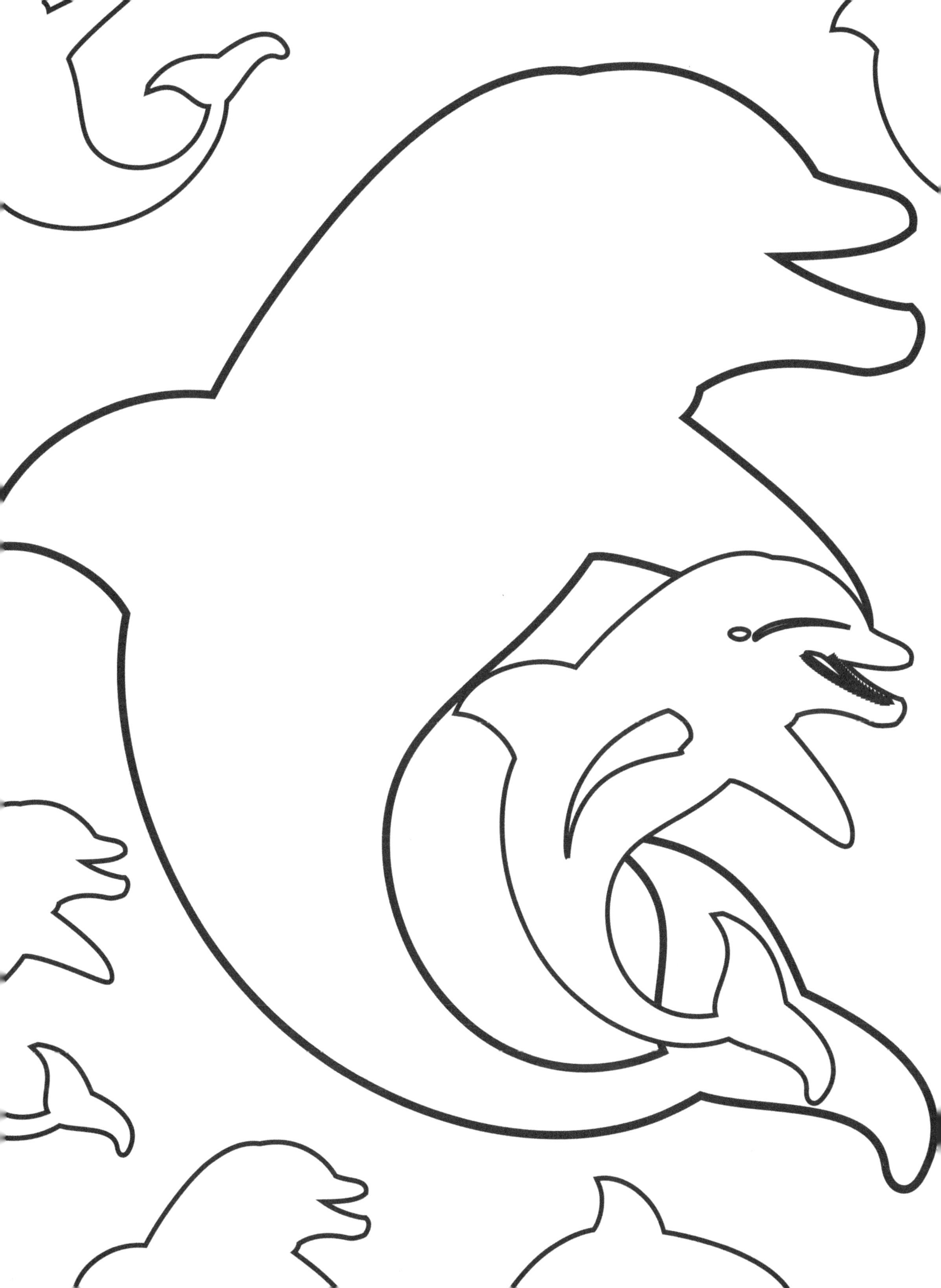

Blotter

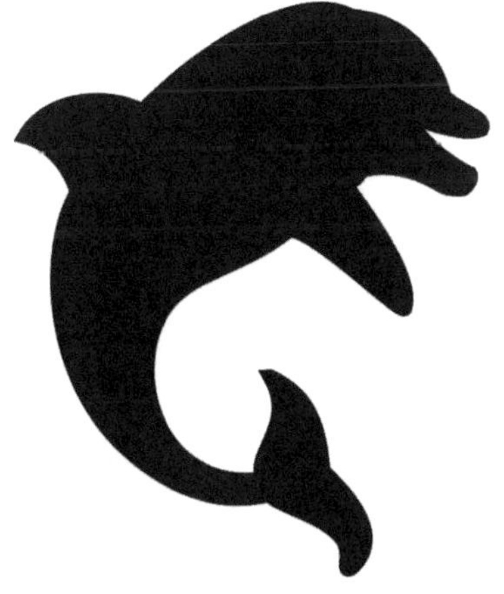

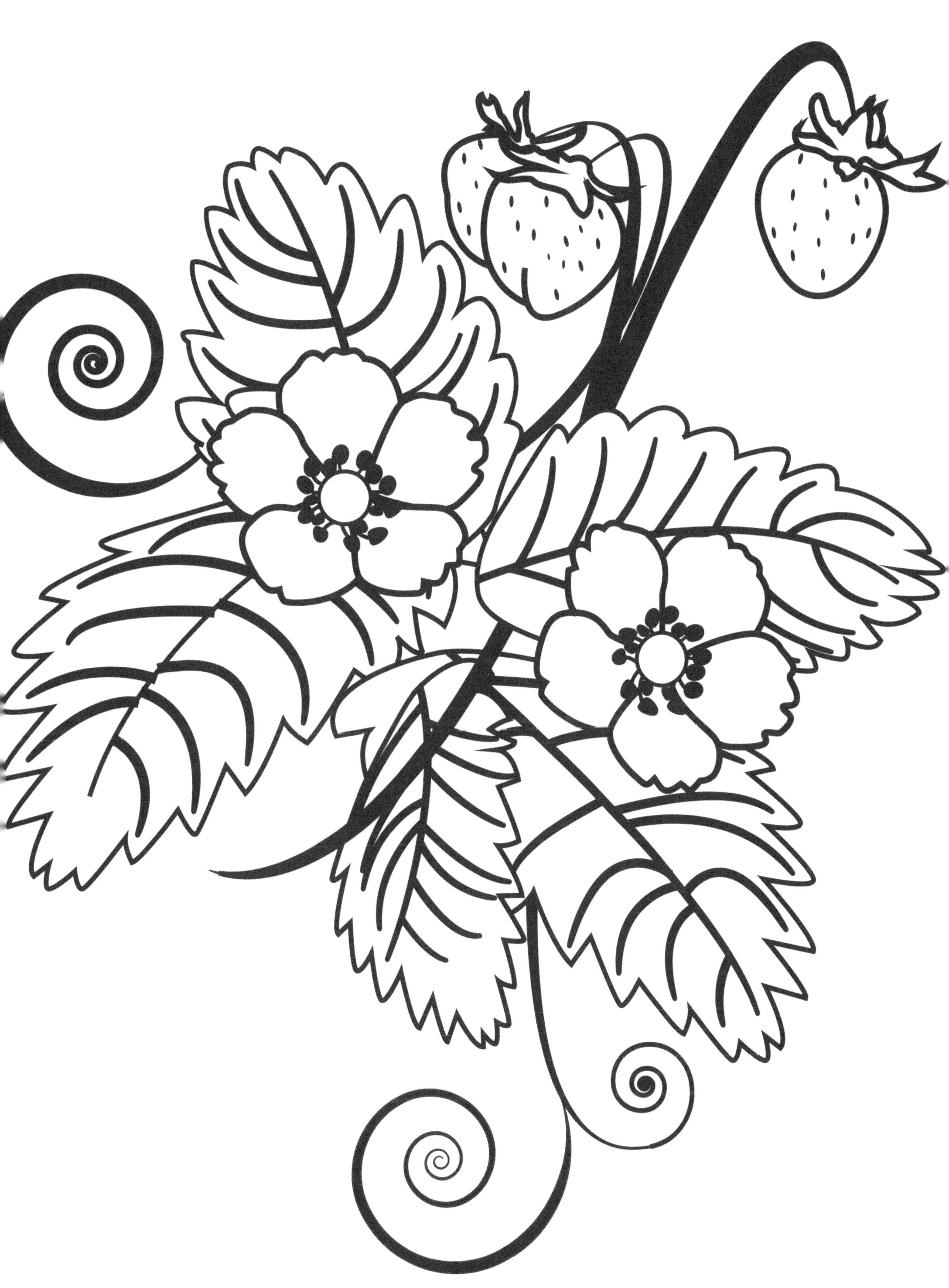

Blotter

Blotter

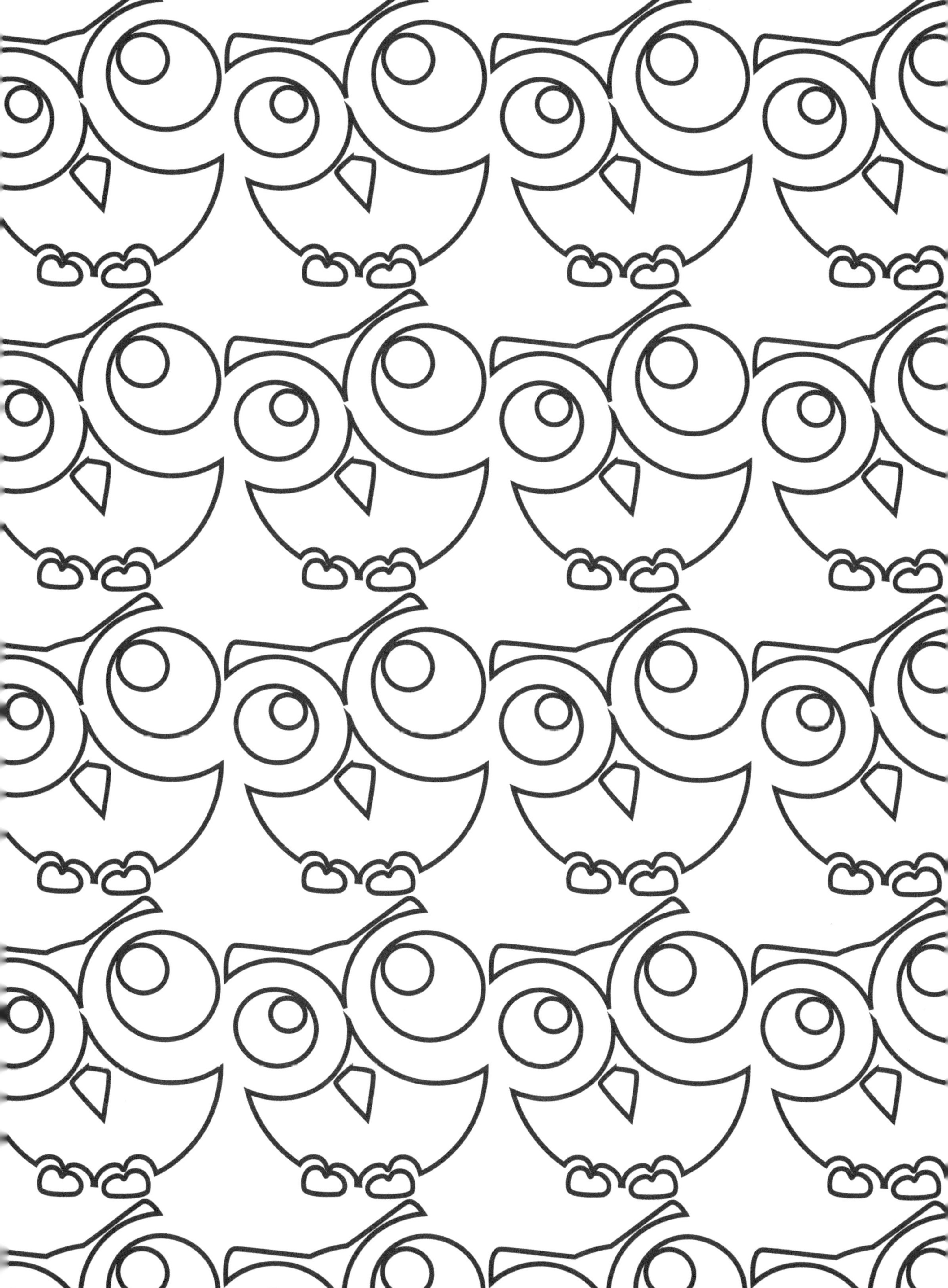

Blotter

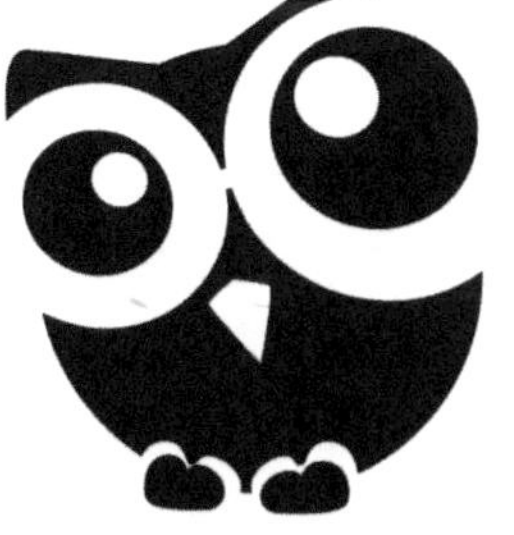

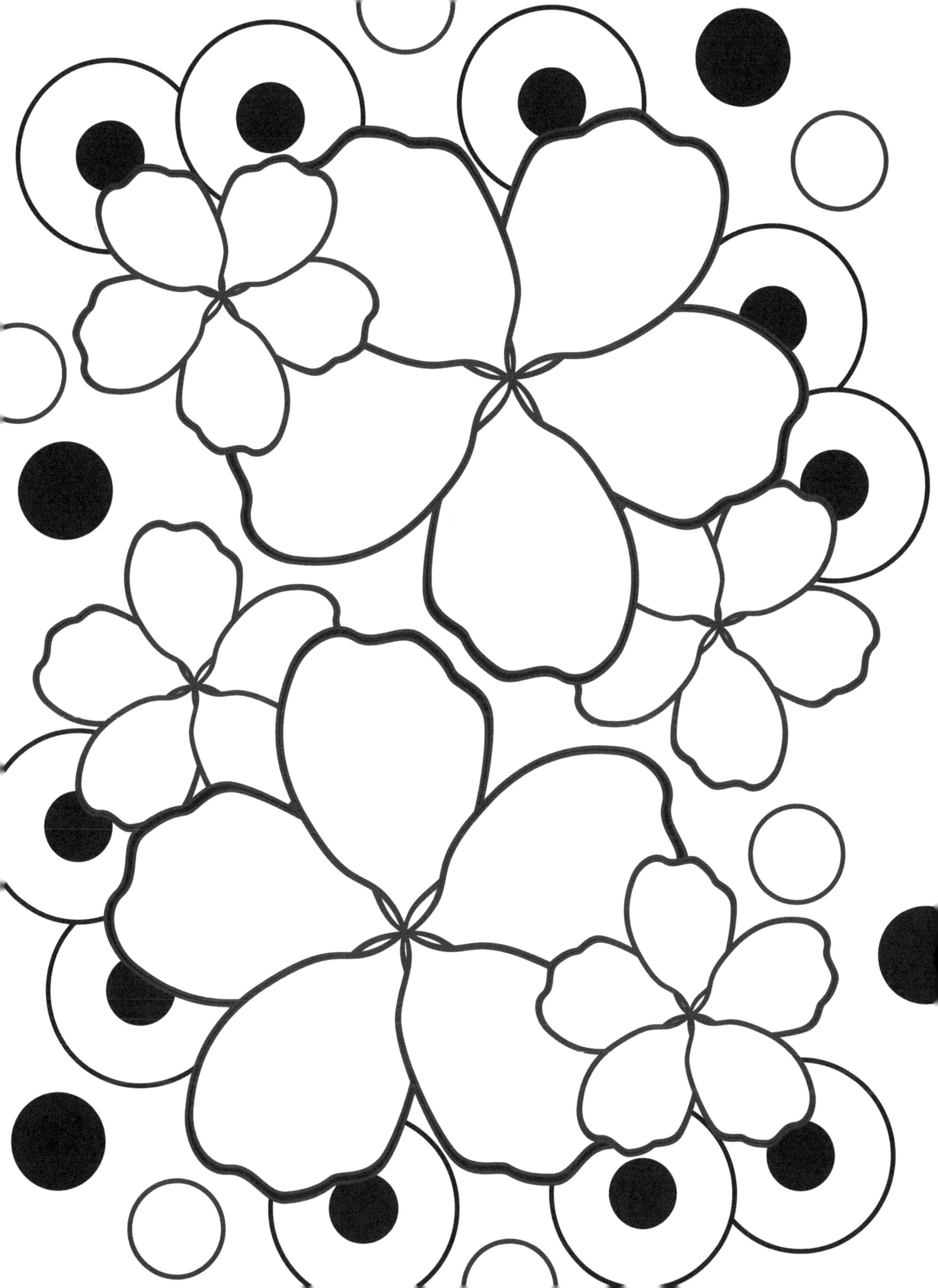

Blotter

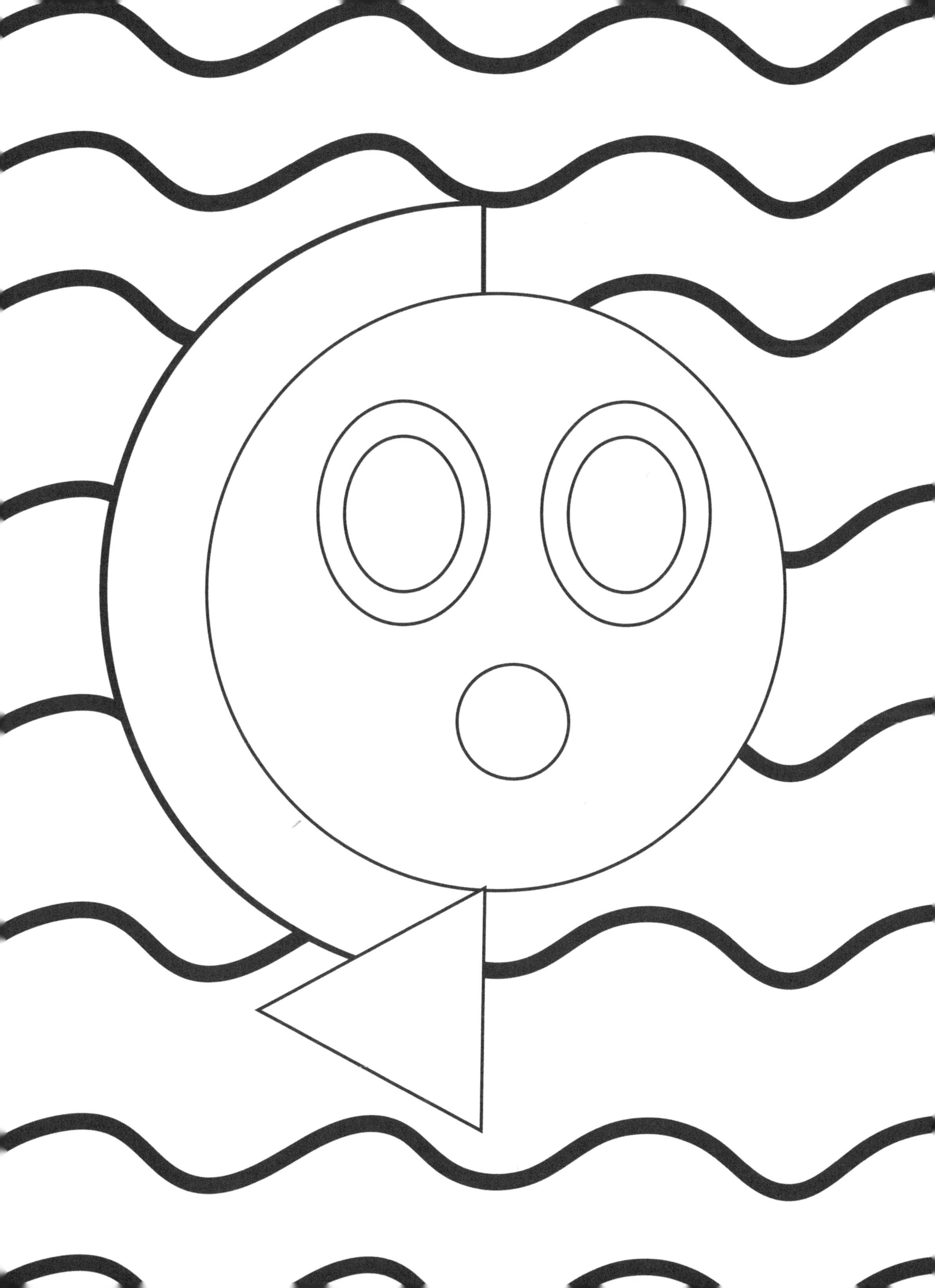

Blotter

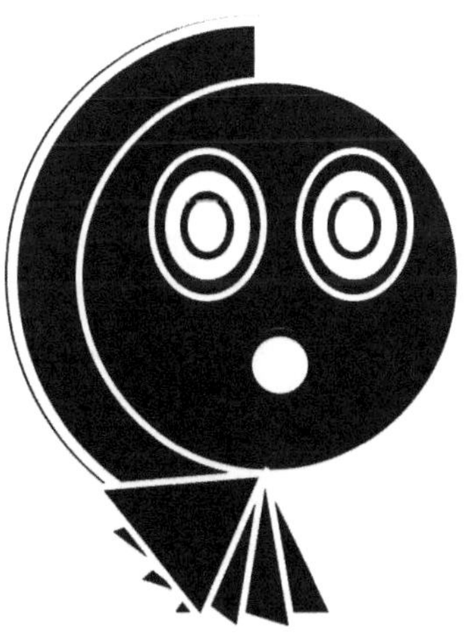

Blotter

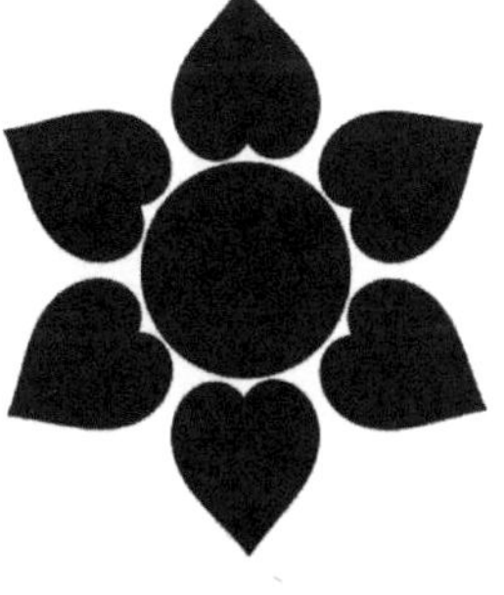

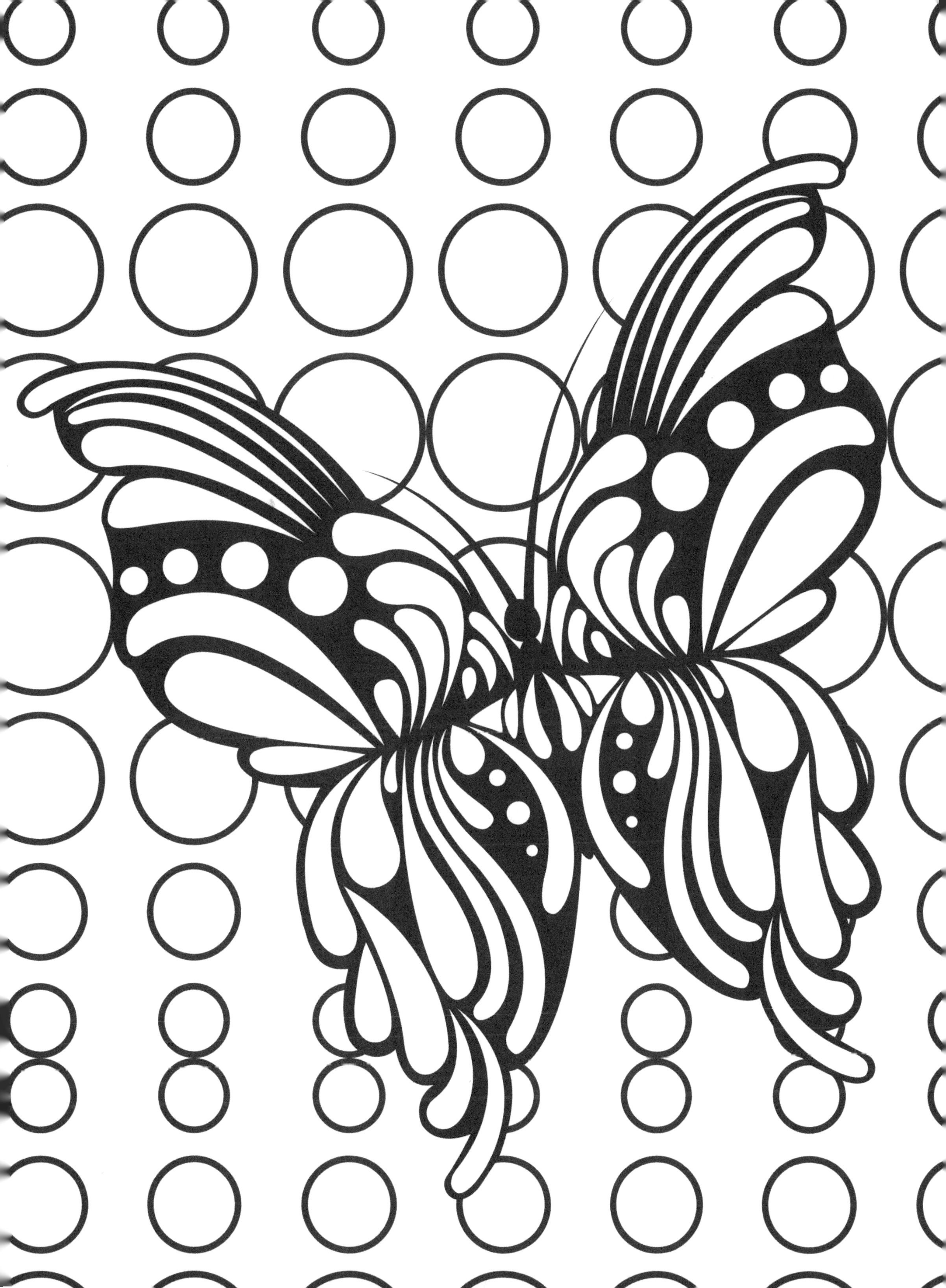

Blotter

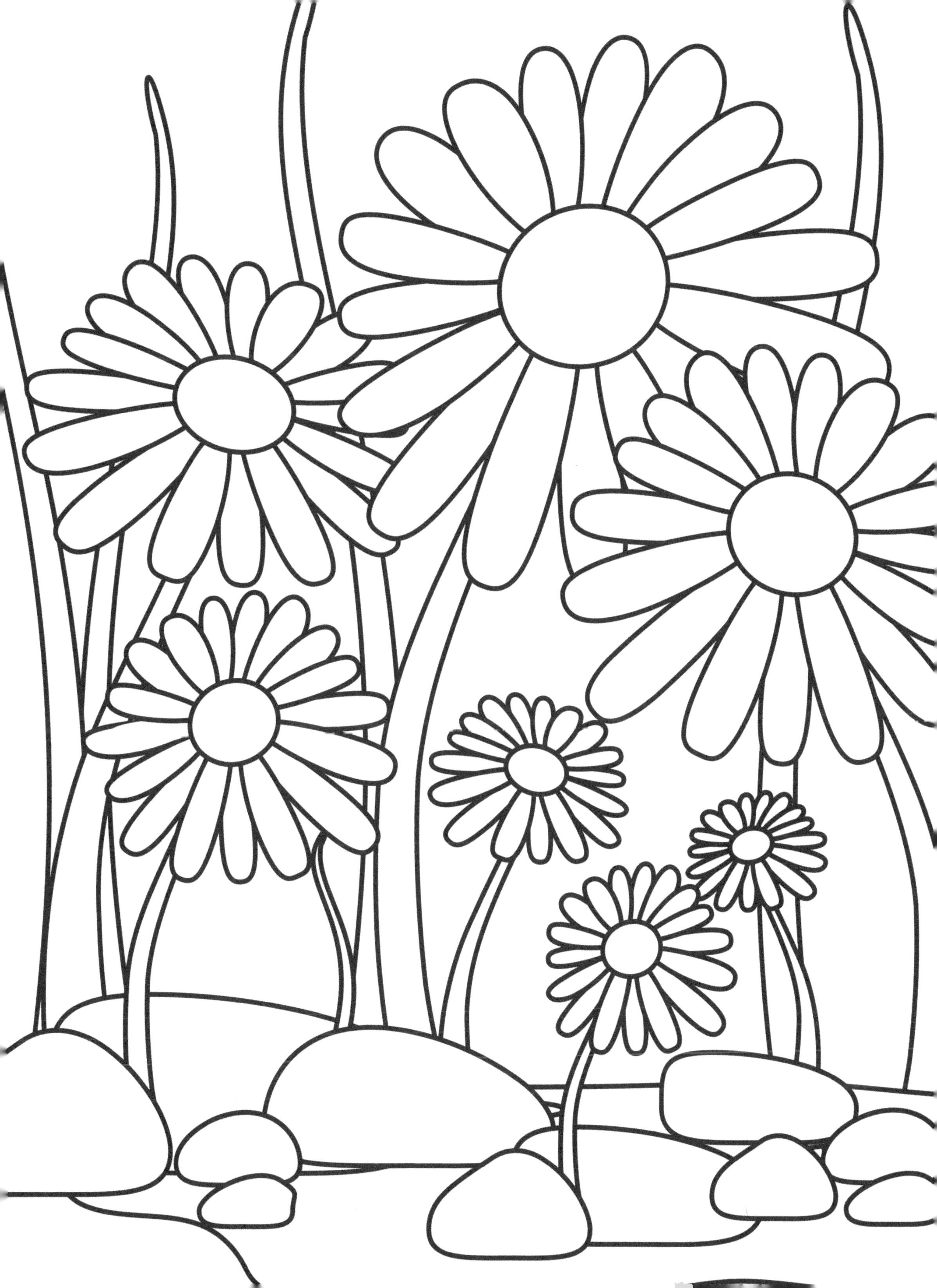

Blotter

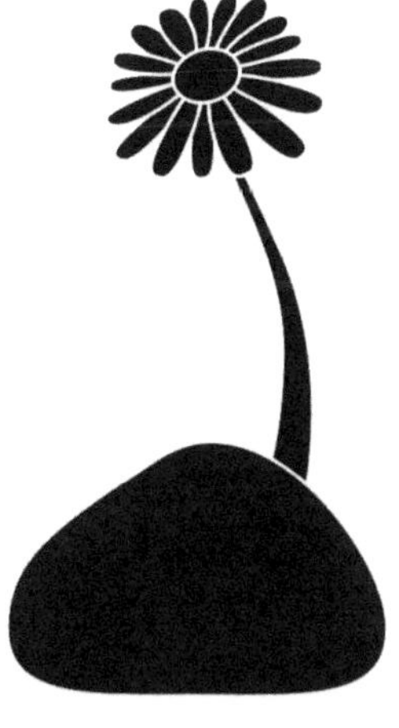

Blotter

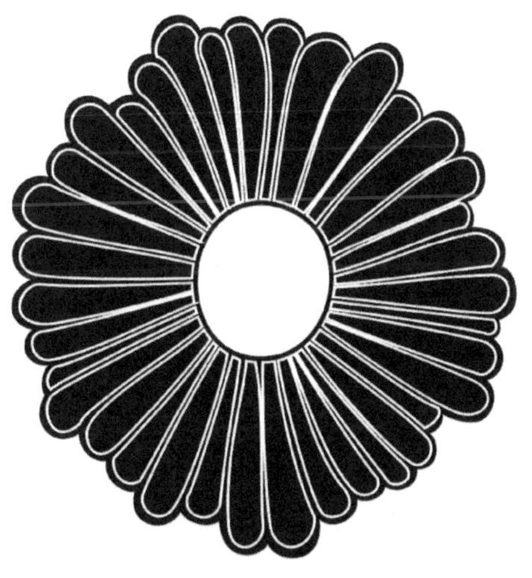

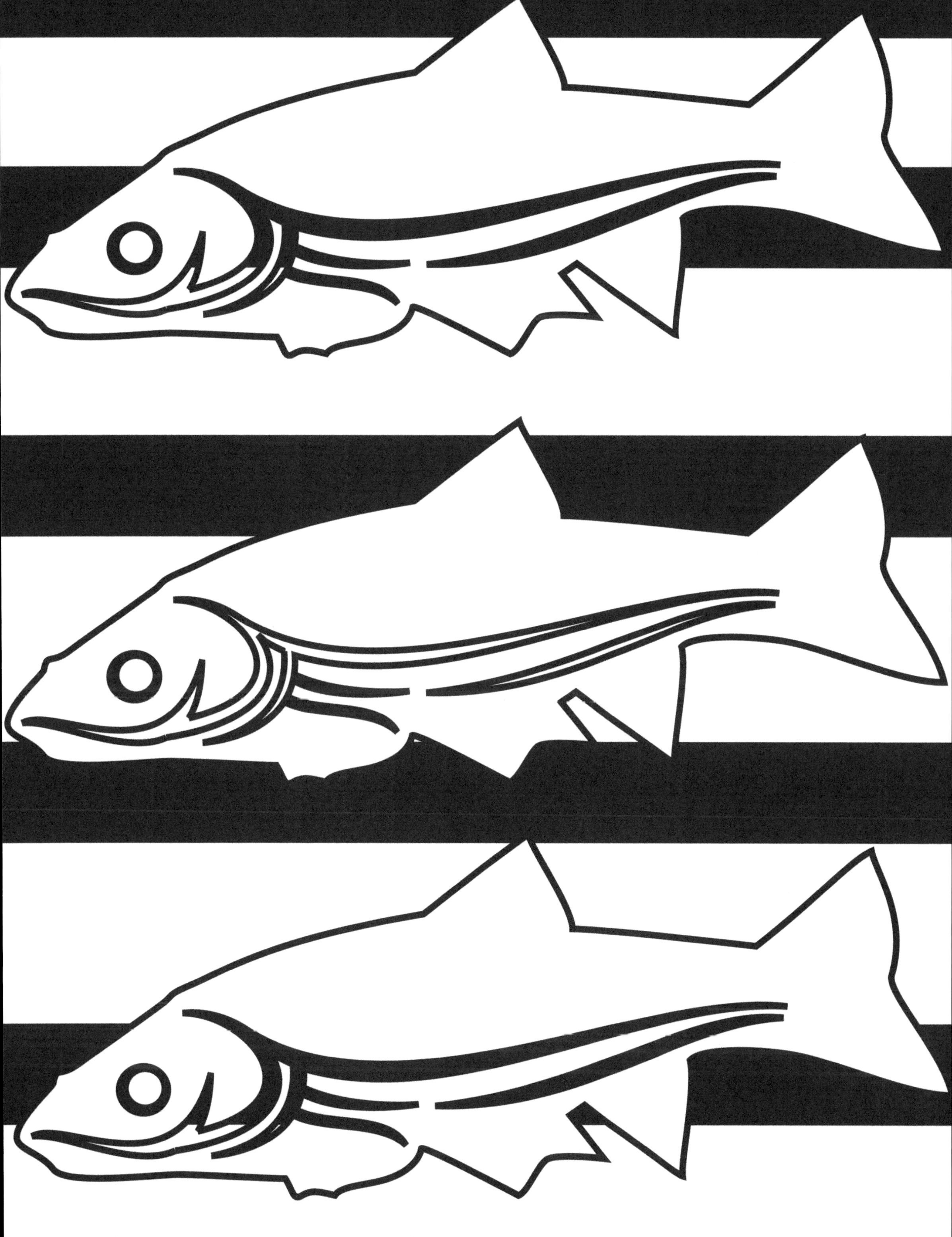

Blotter

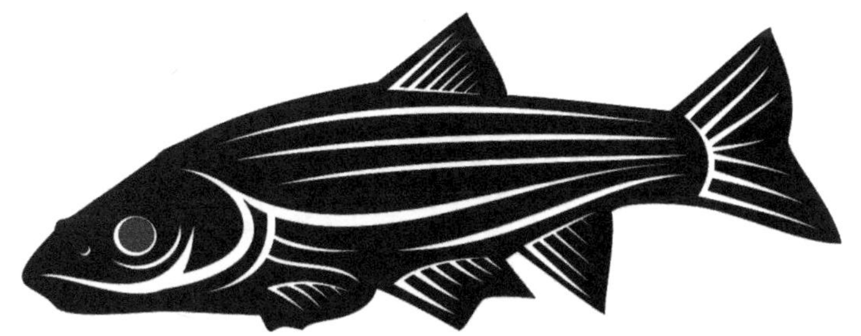

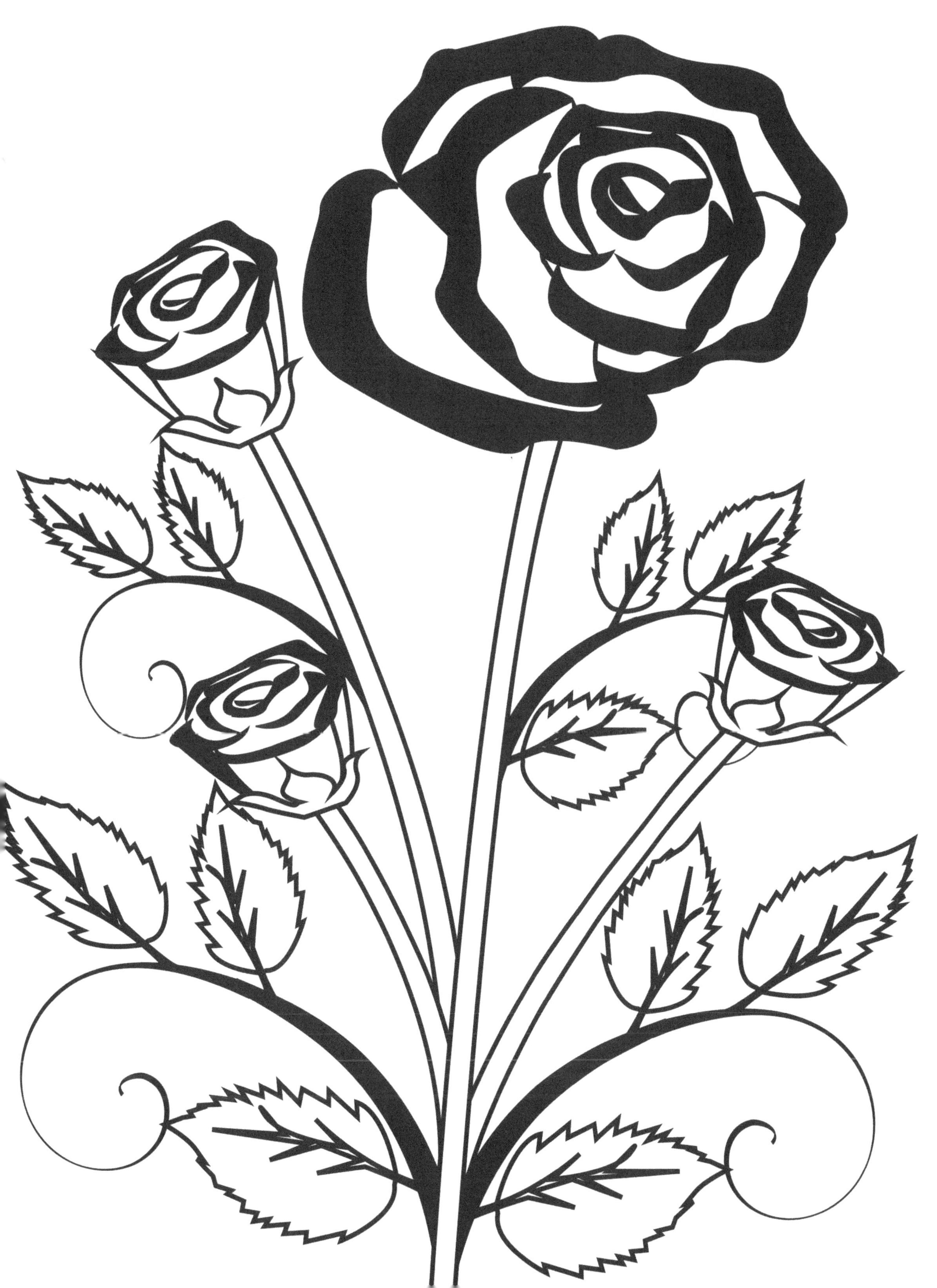

Blotter

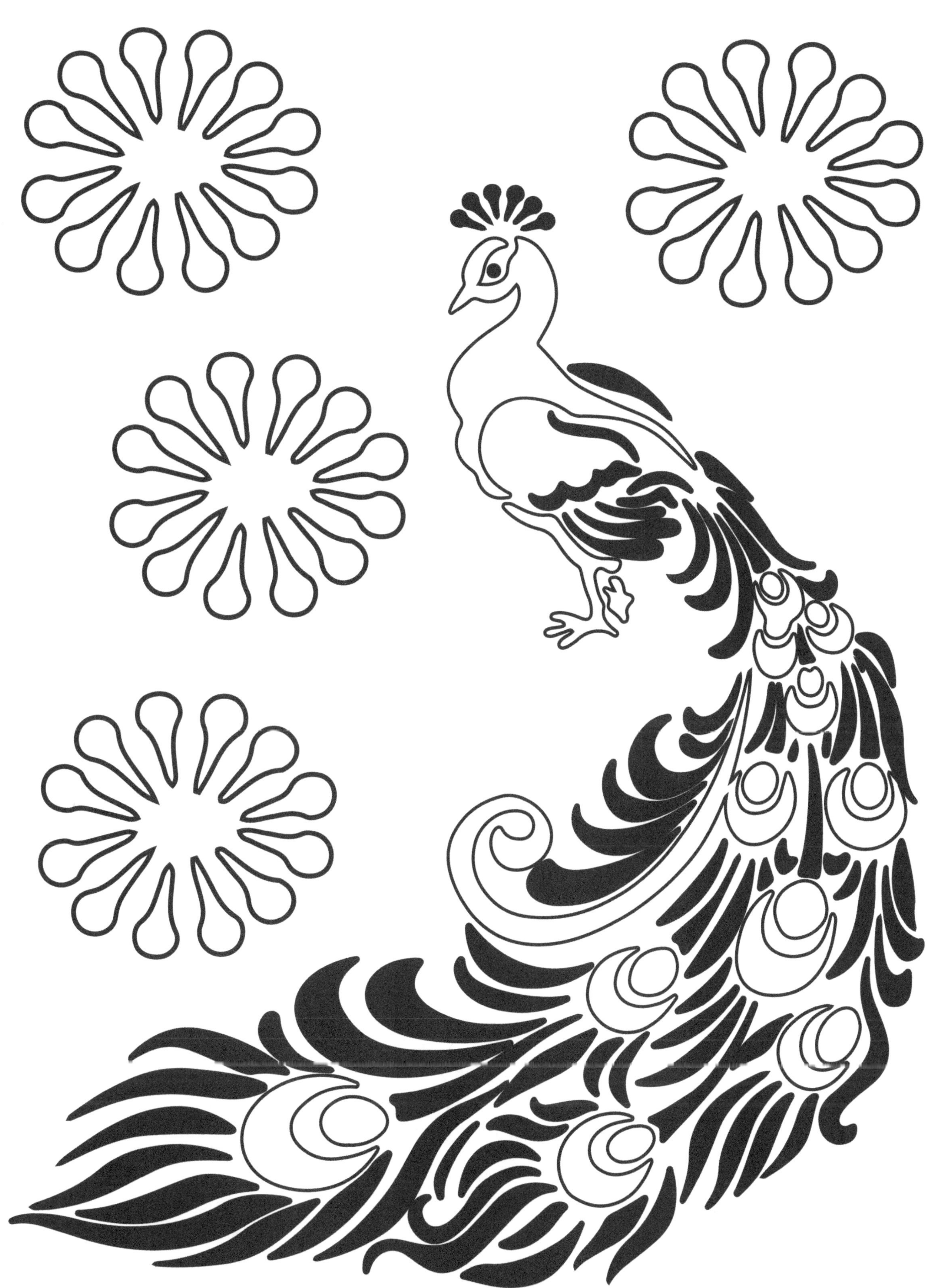

Blotter

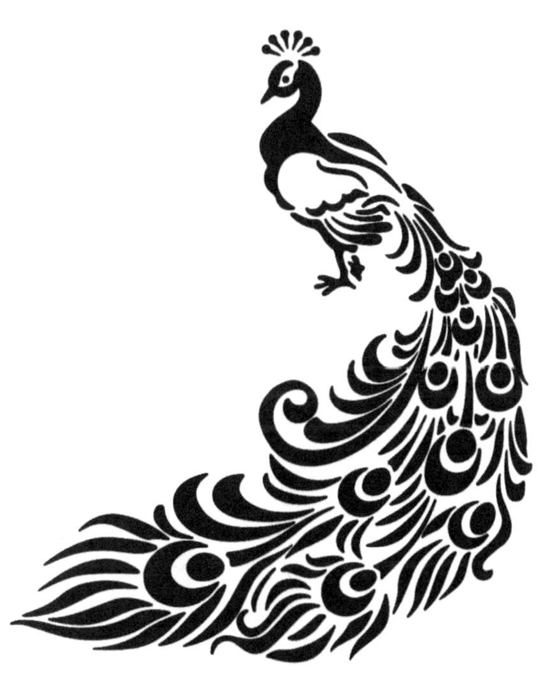

Blotter

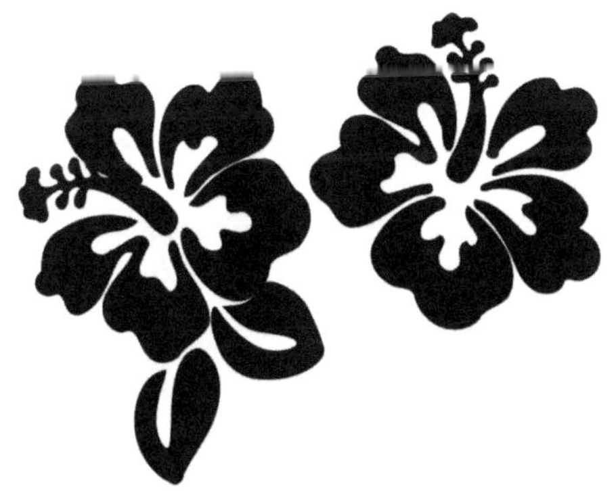

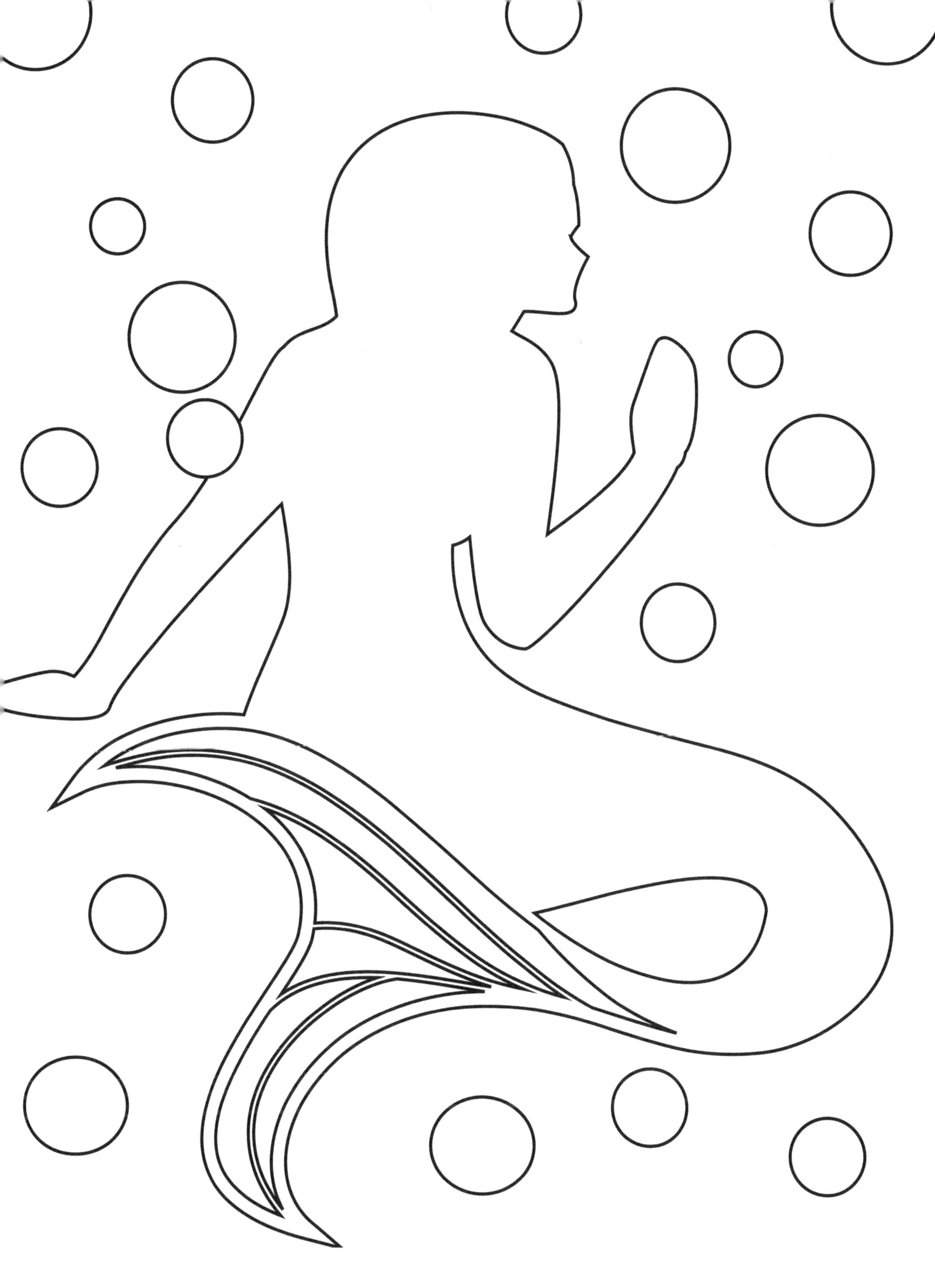

Blotter

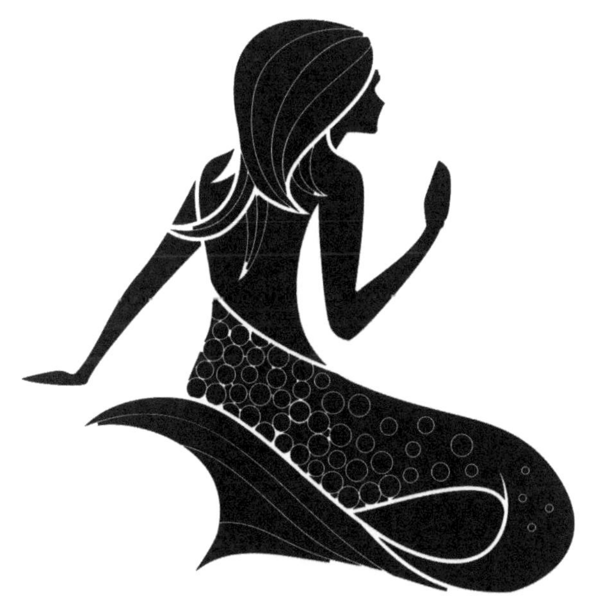

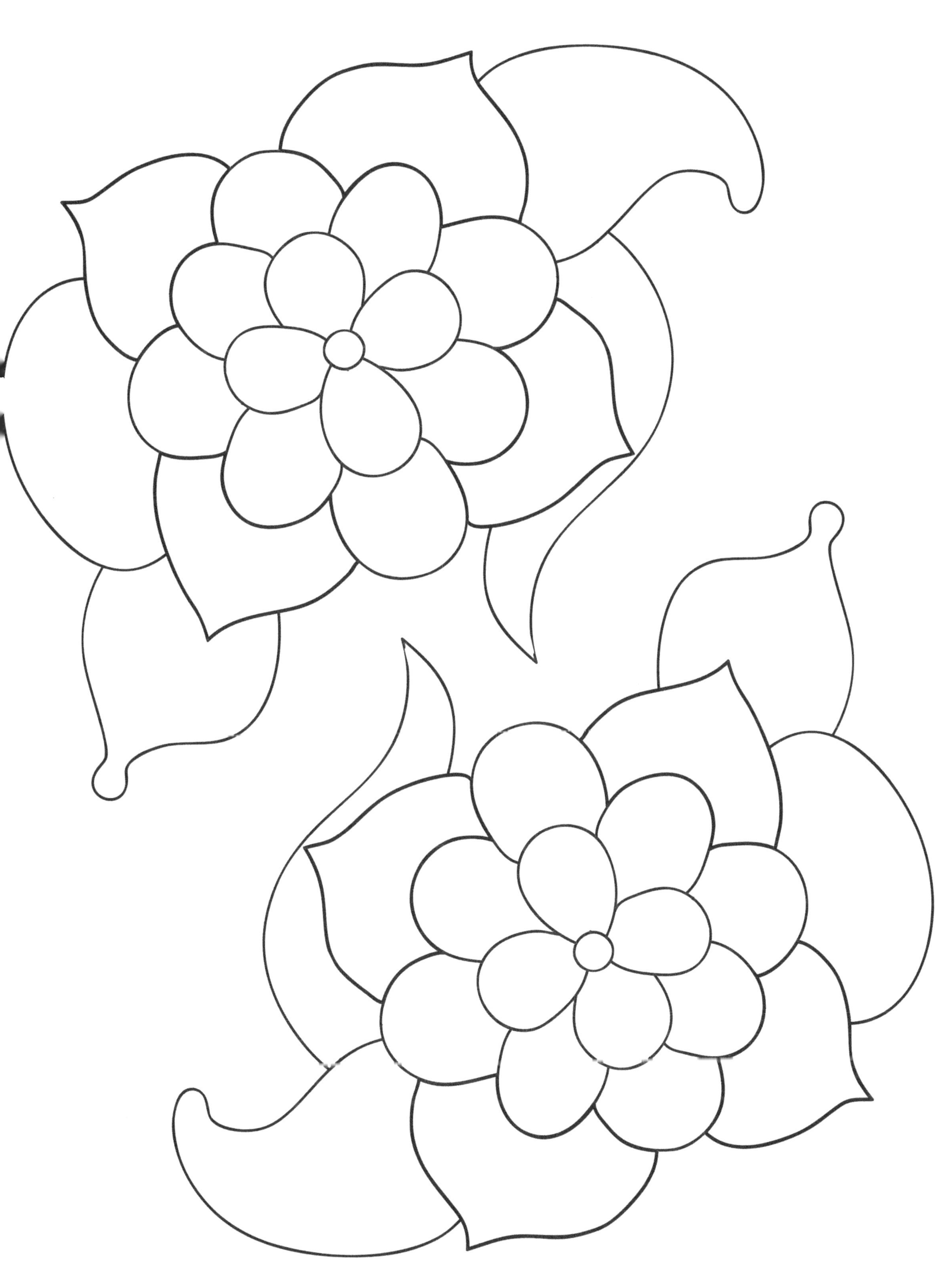

Blotter

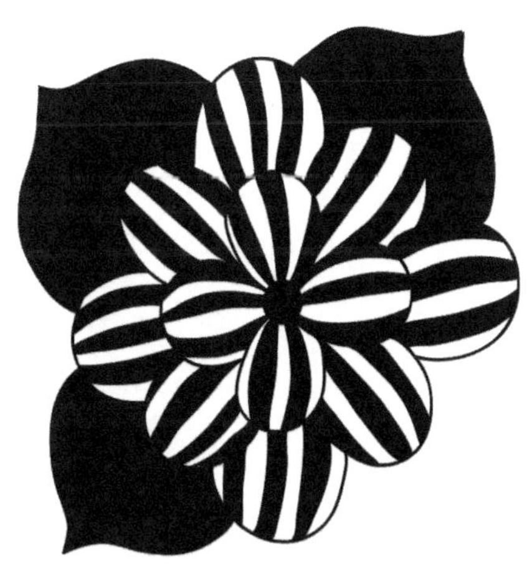

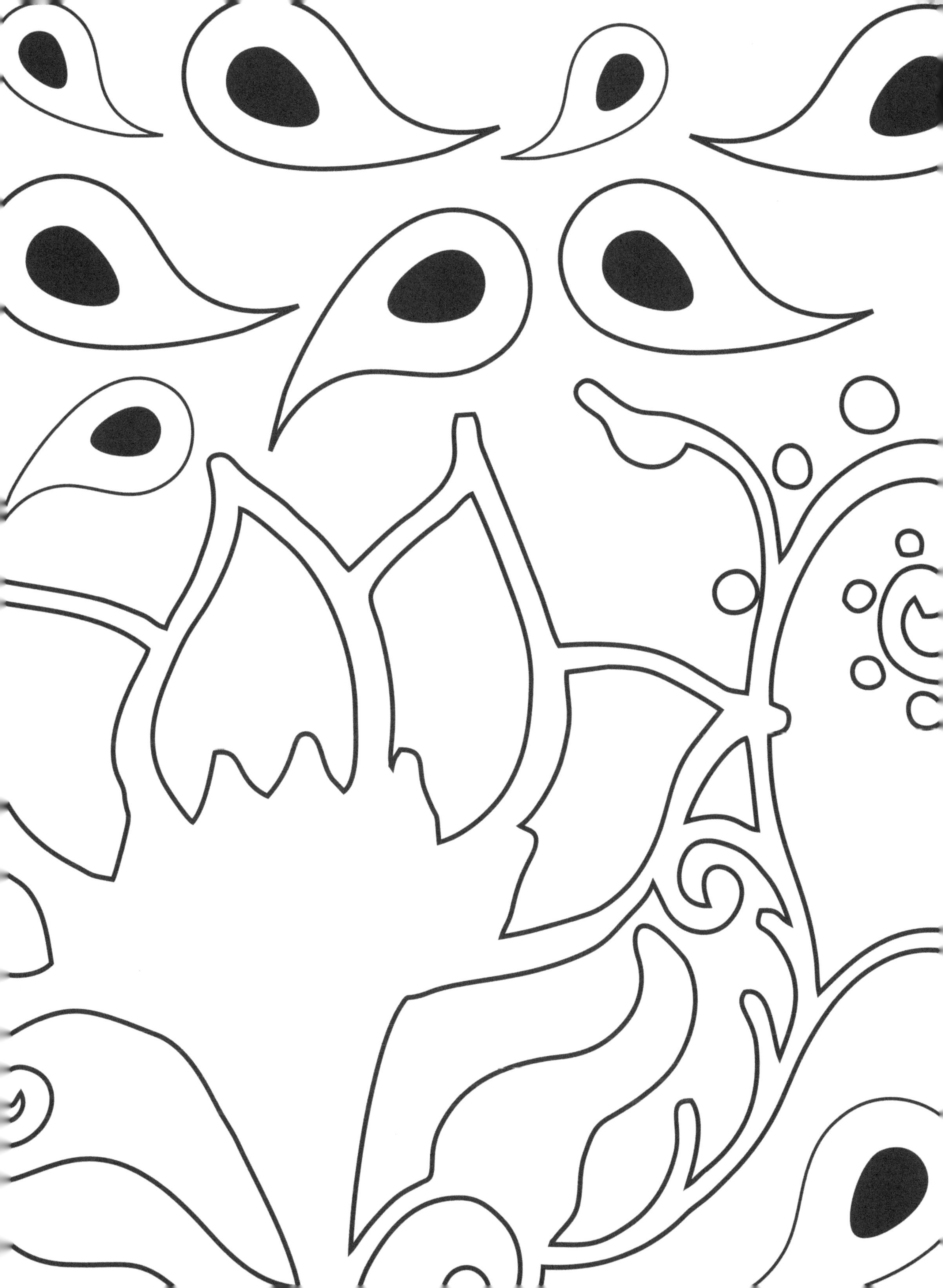

Blotter

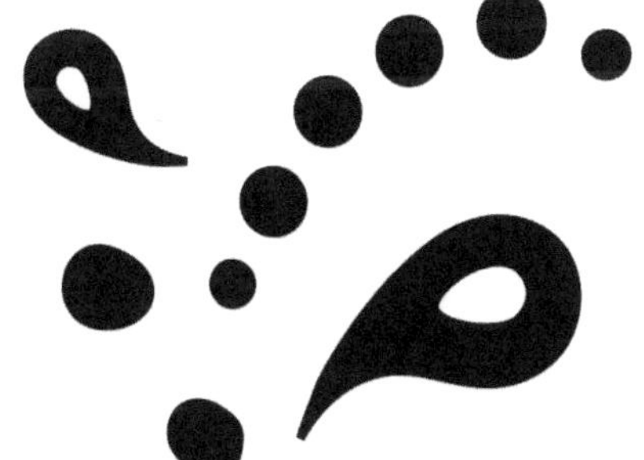

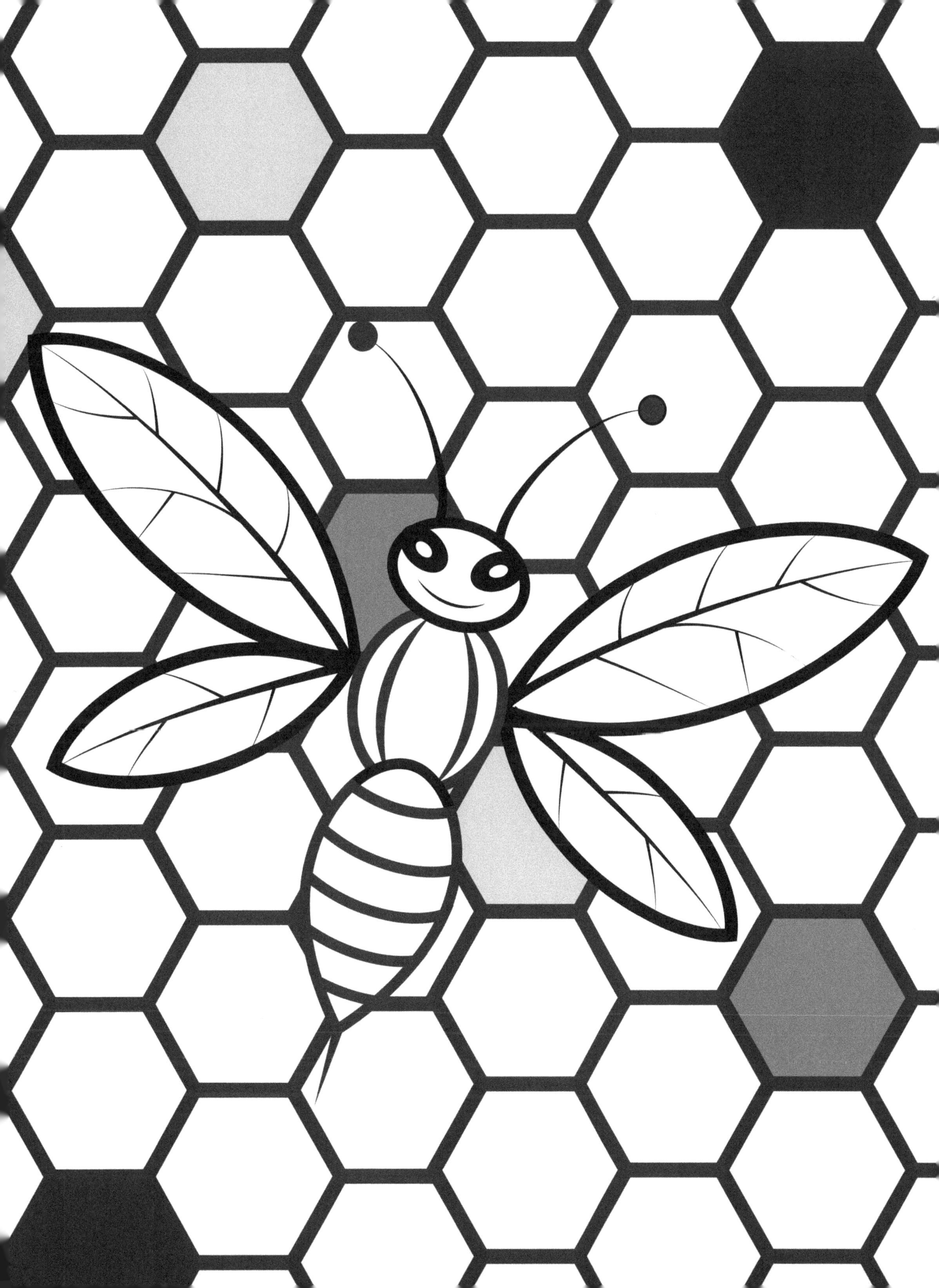

Blotter

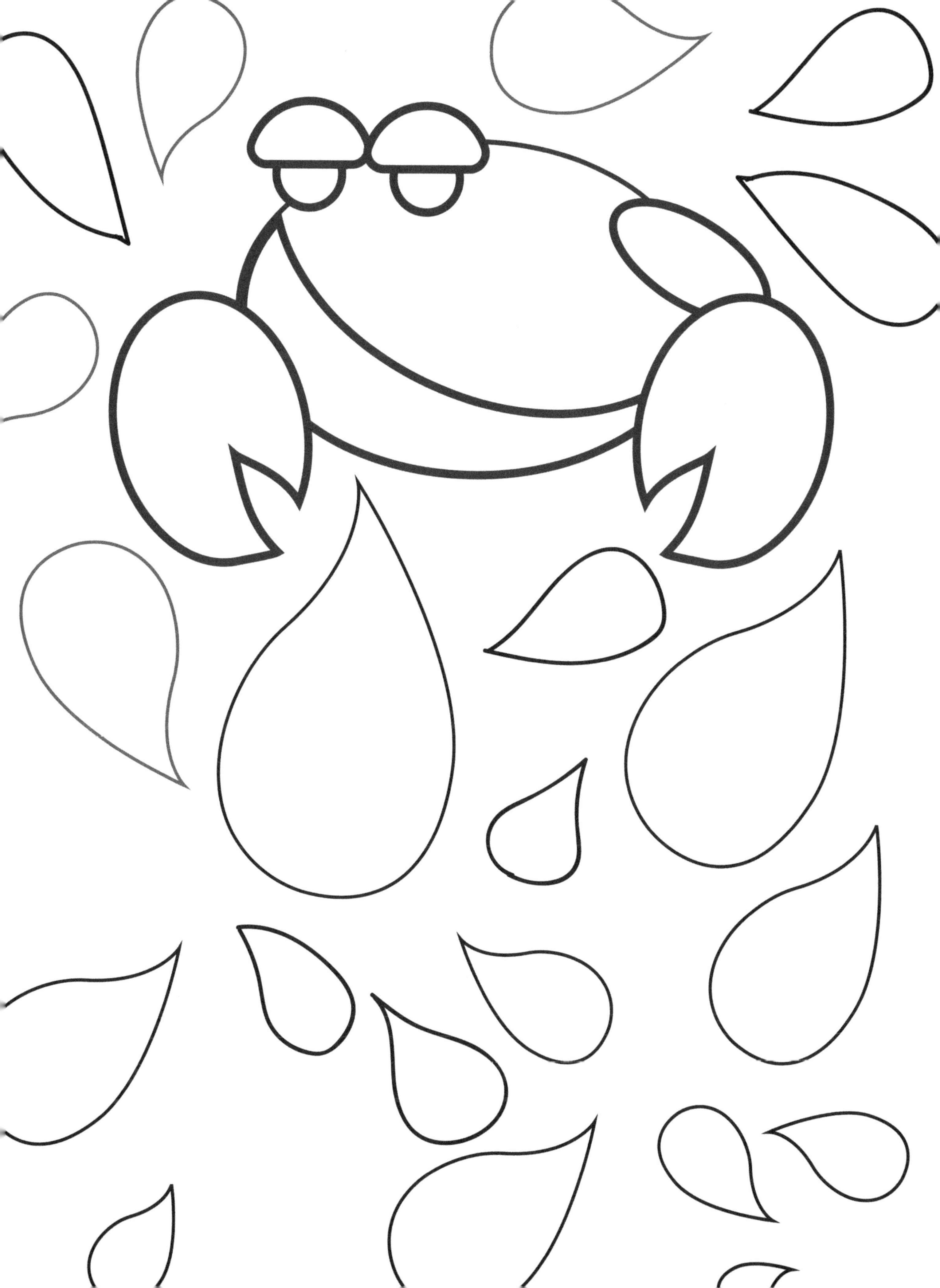

Blotter

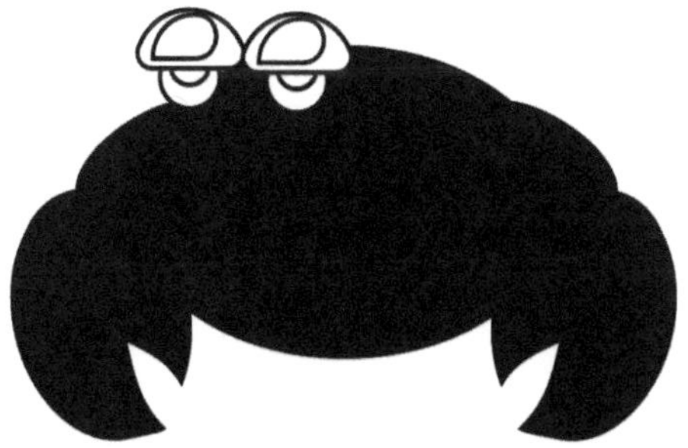

Blotter

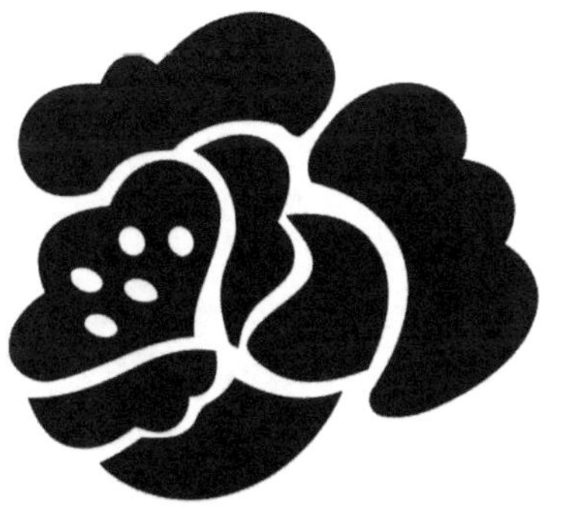

Blotter

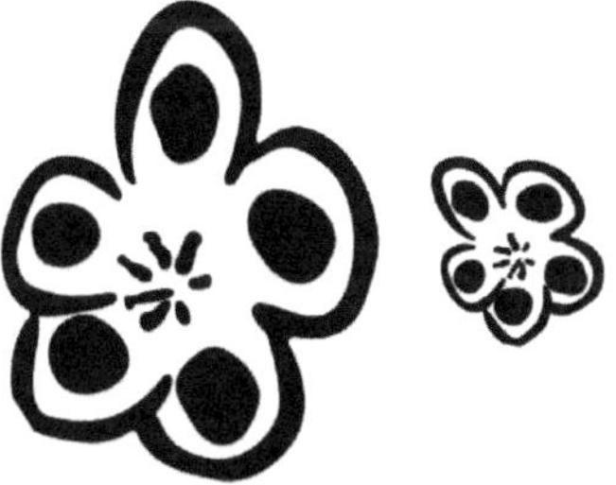

Blotter

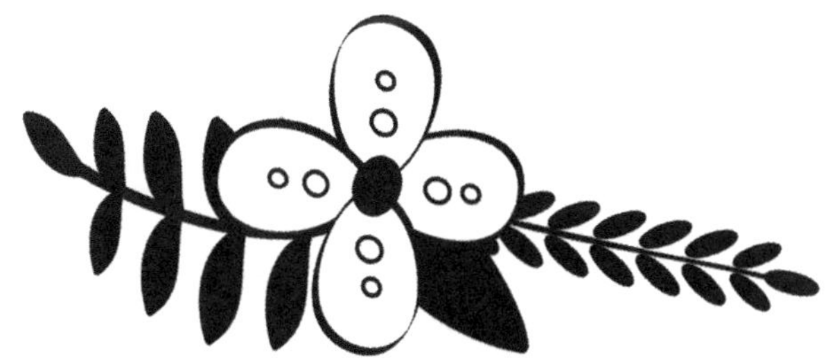

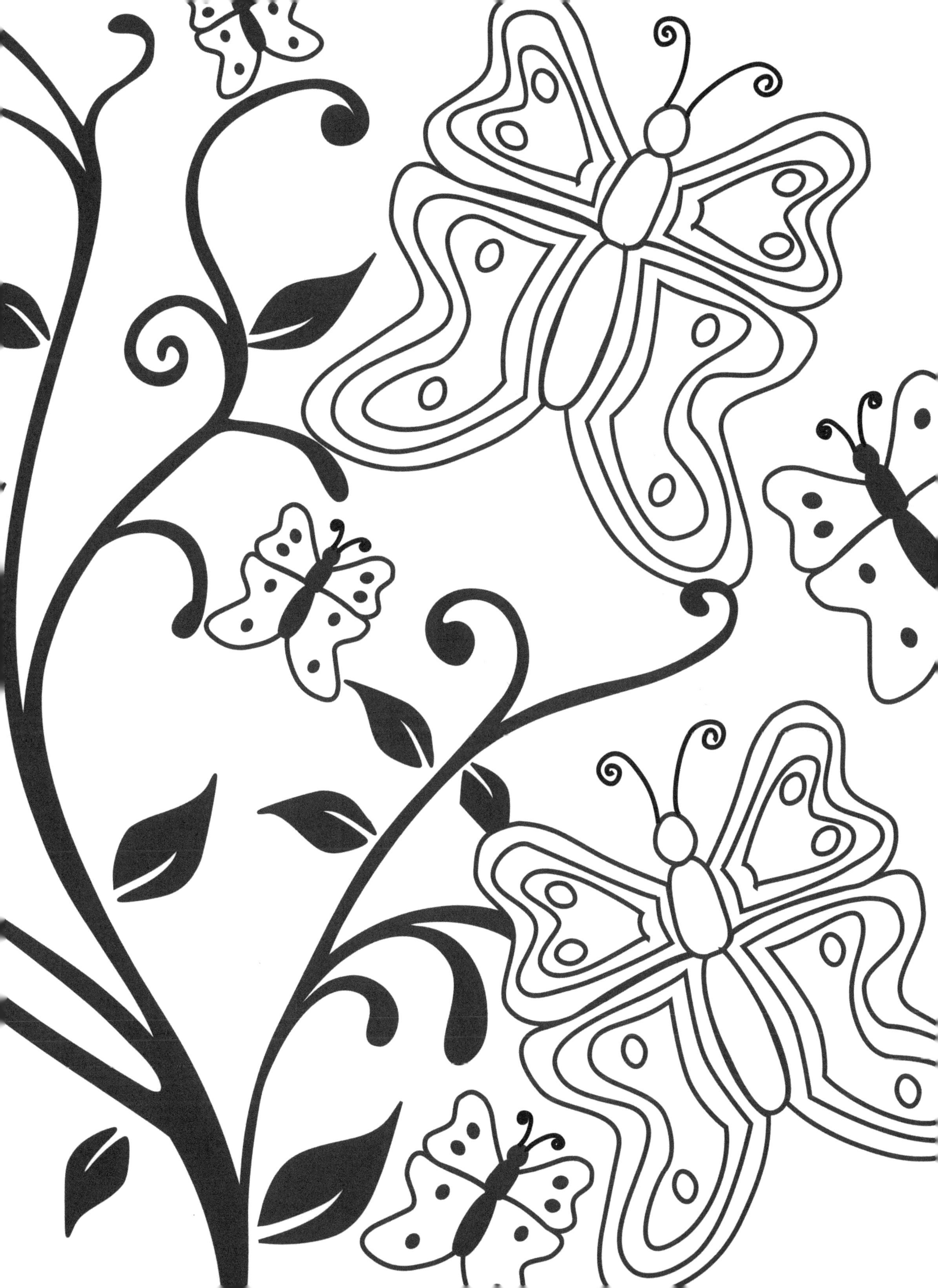

Blotter

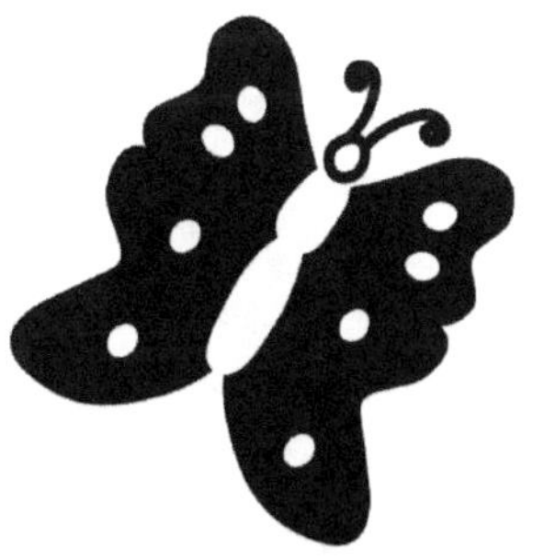

Blotter

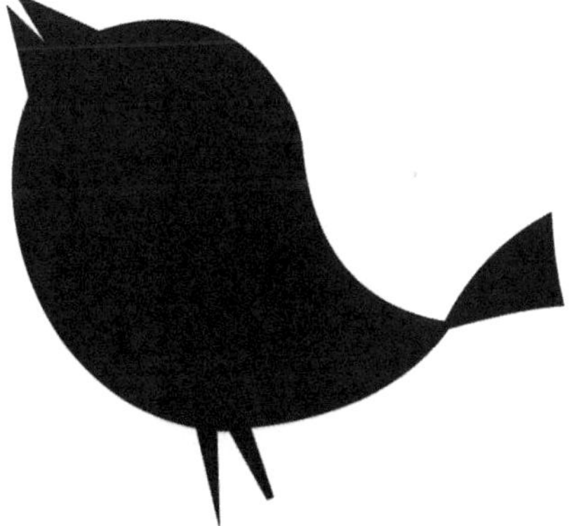

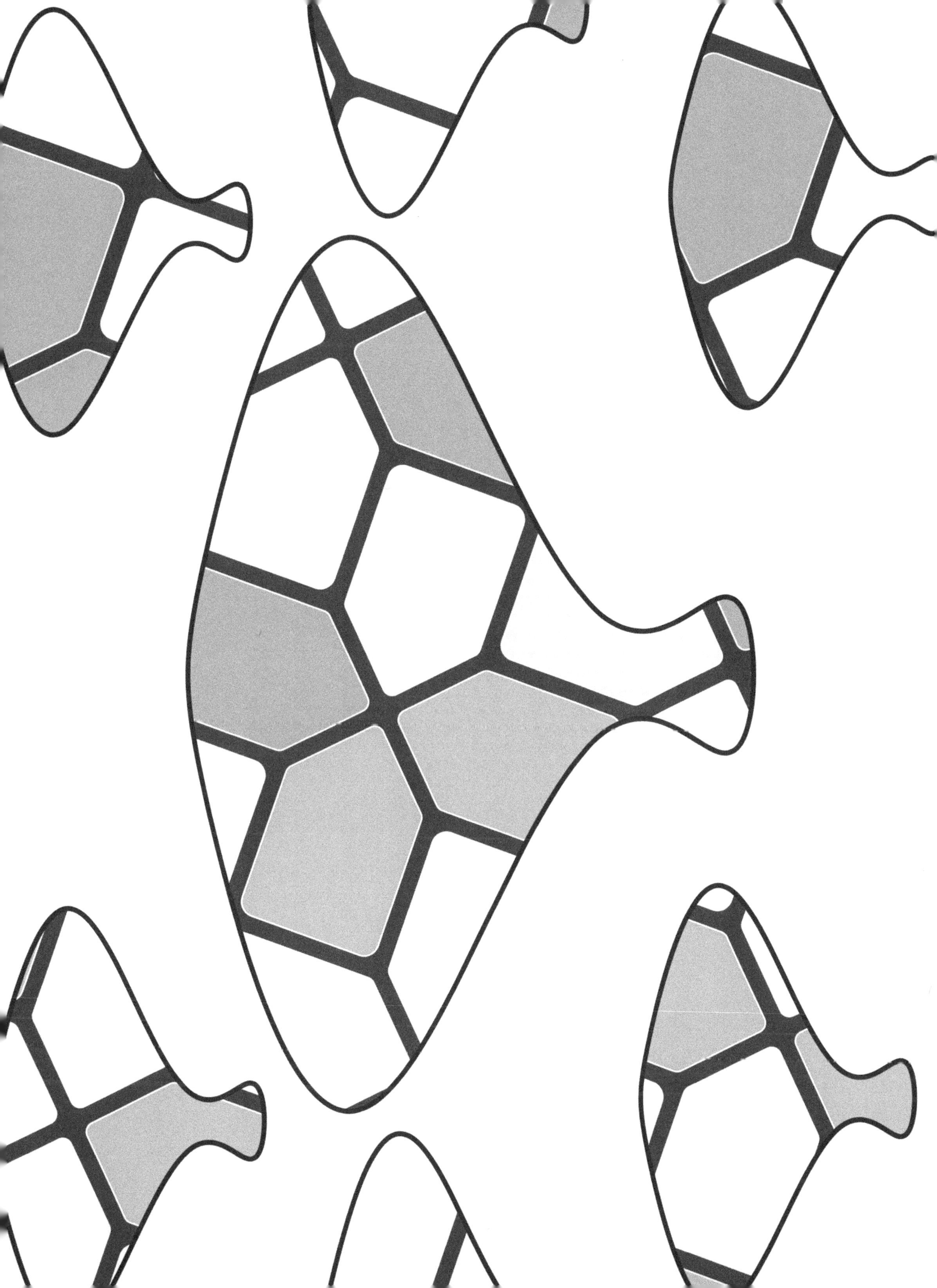

Blotter

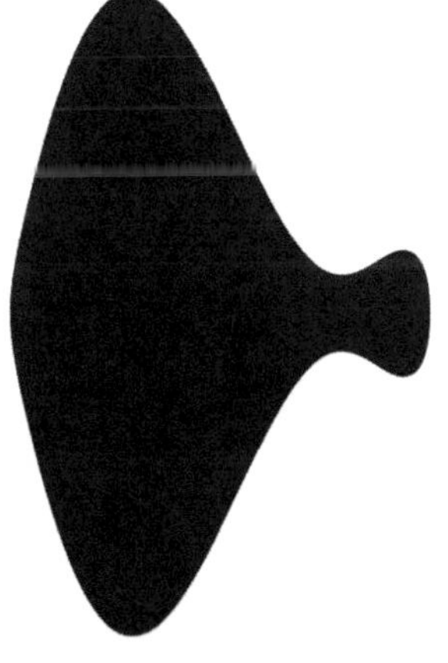

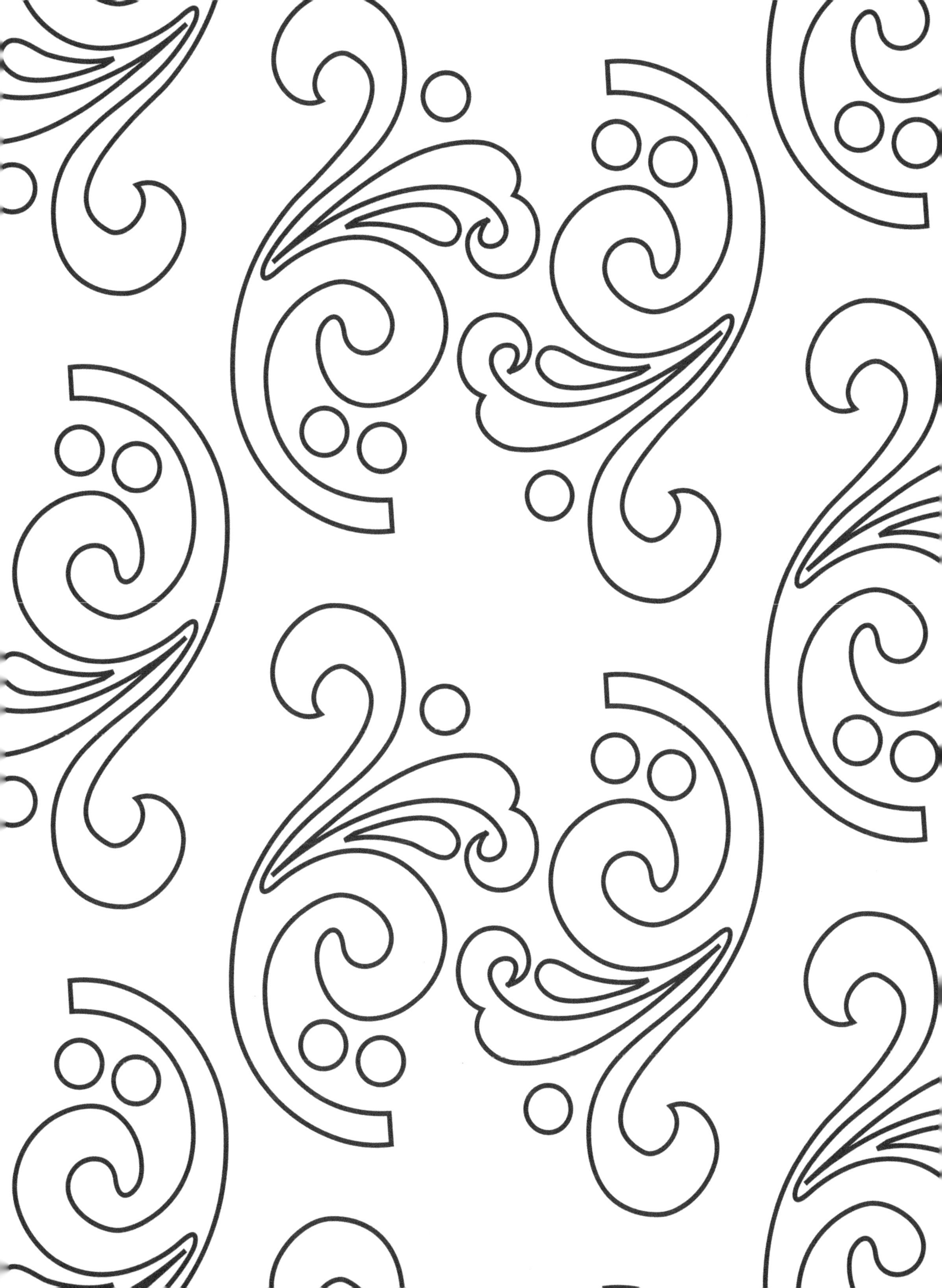

Blotter

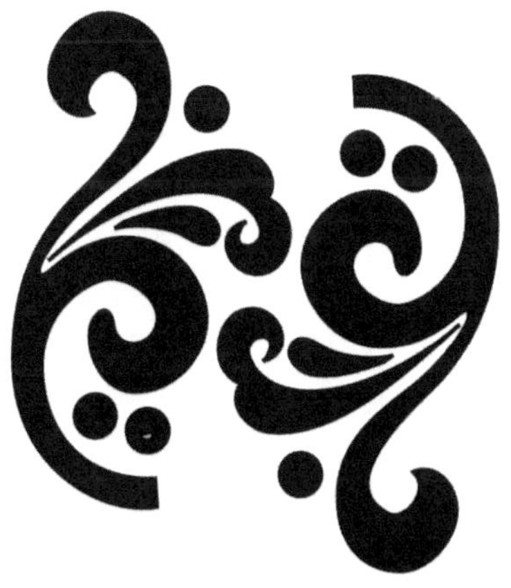

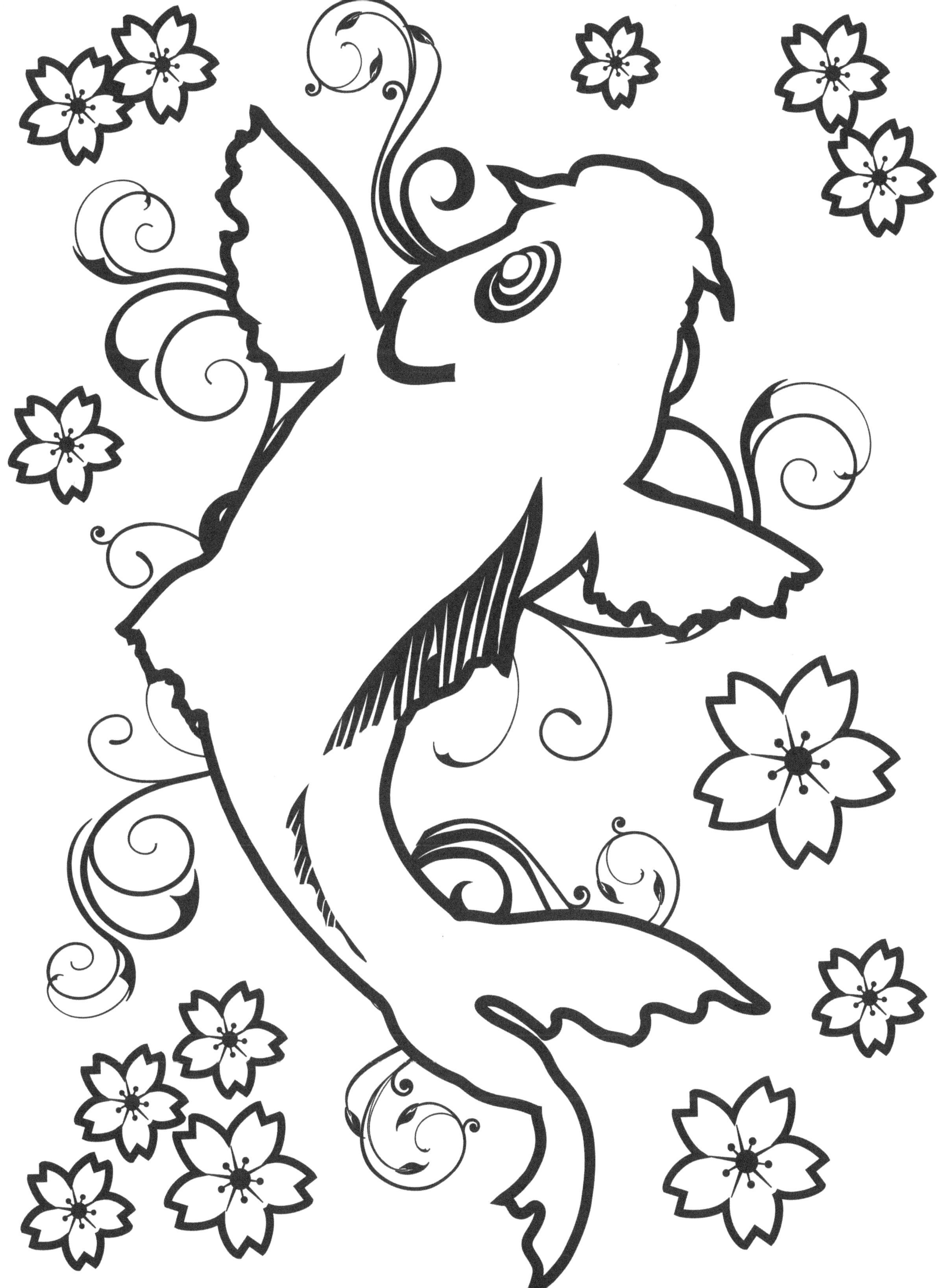

Blotter

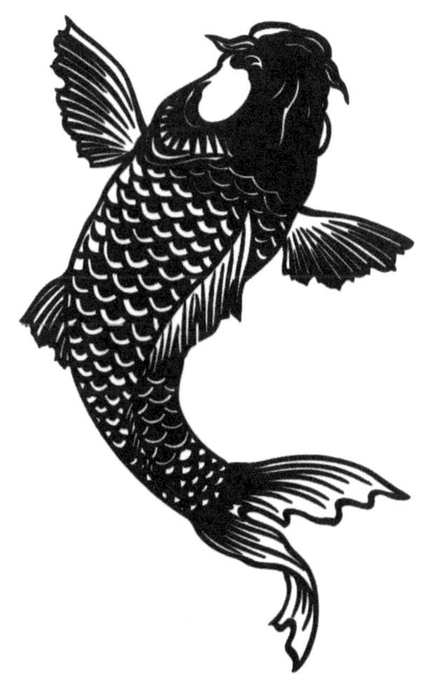

Blotter

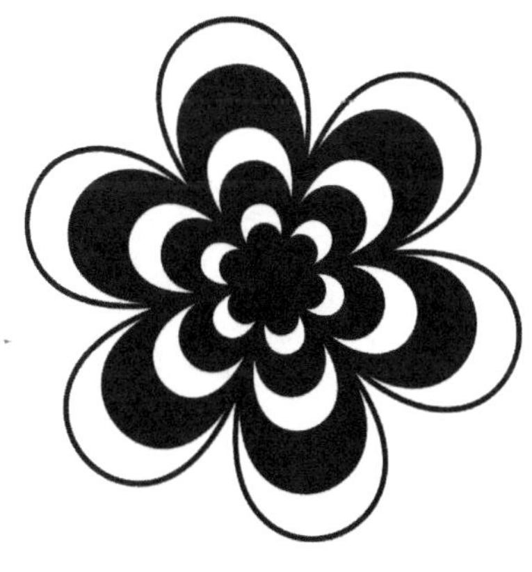

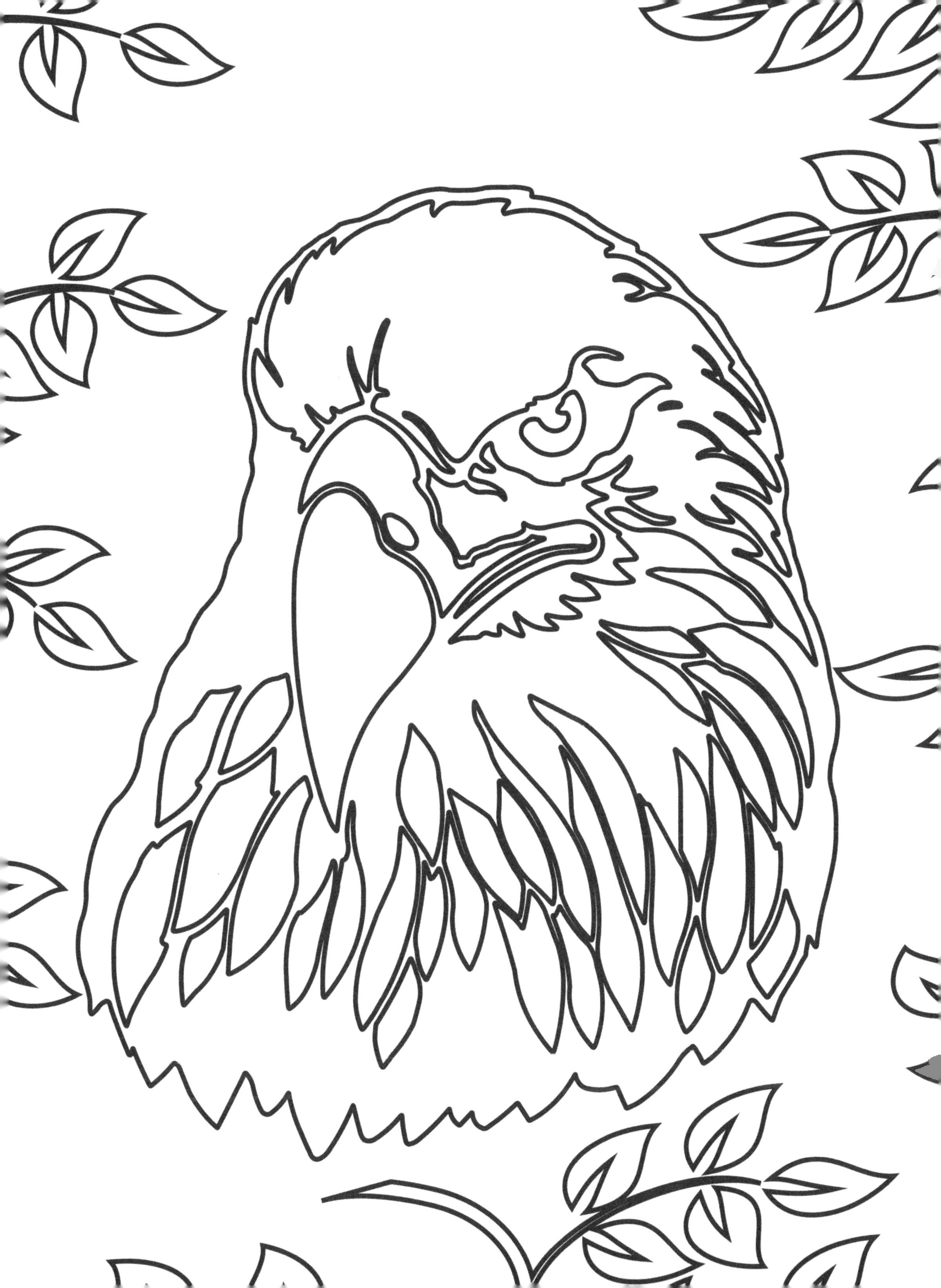

Blotter

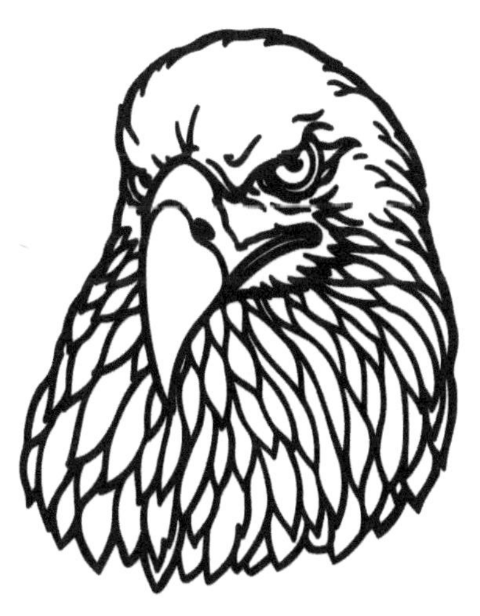

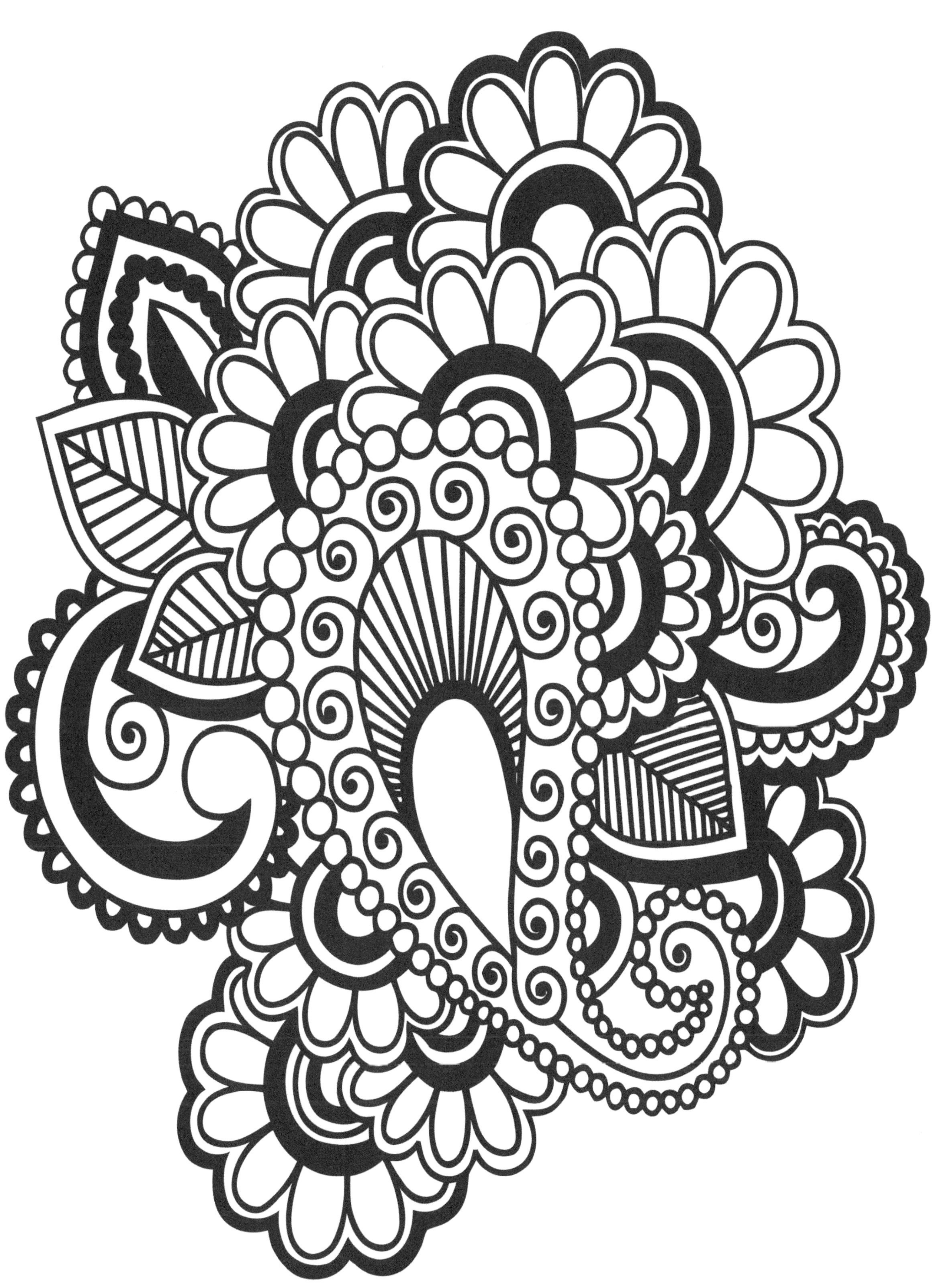

Blotter

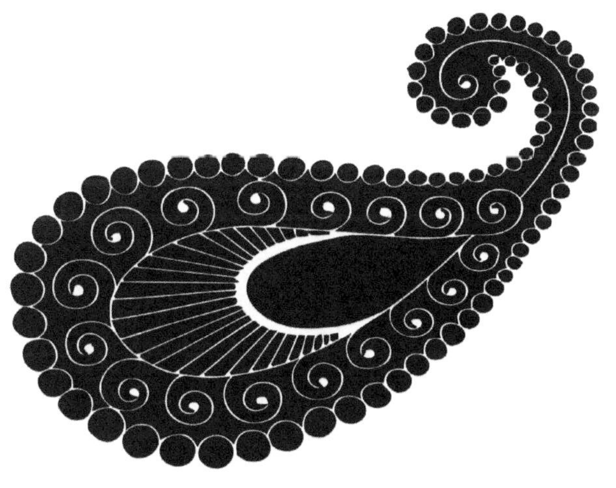

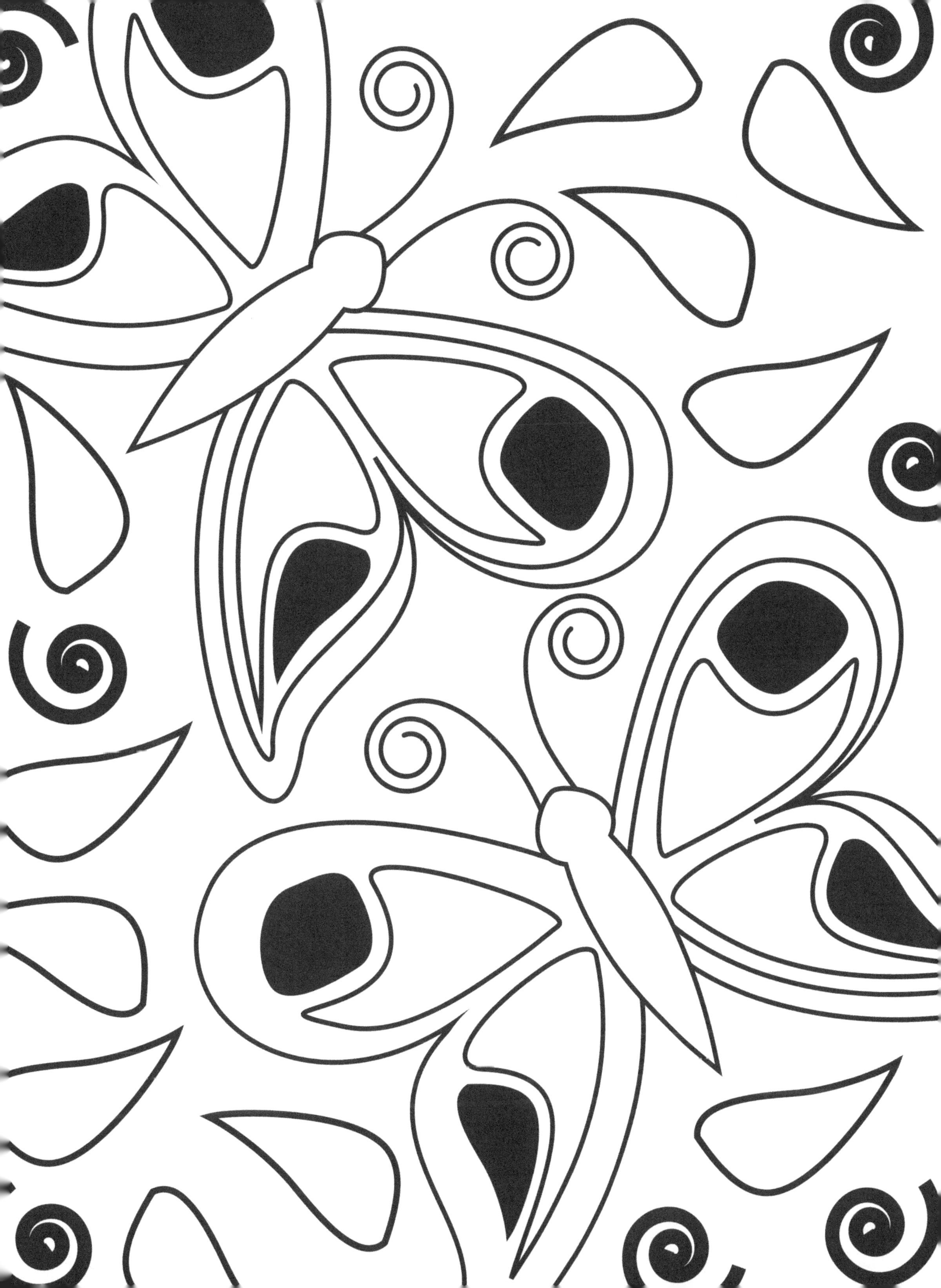

Blotter

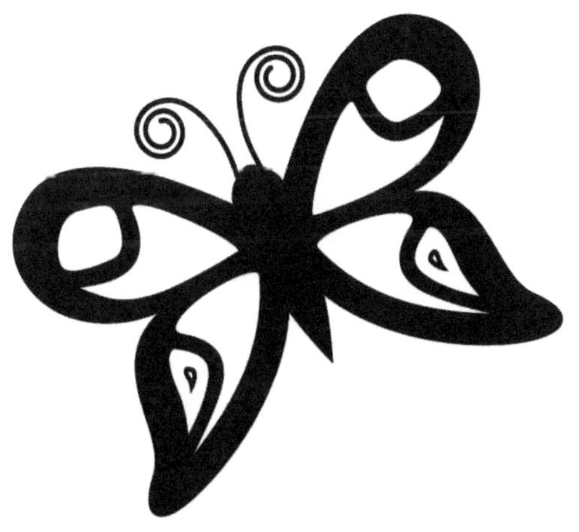

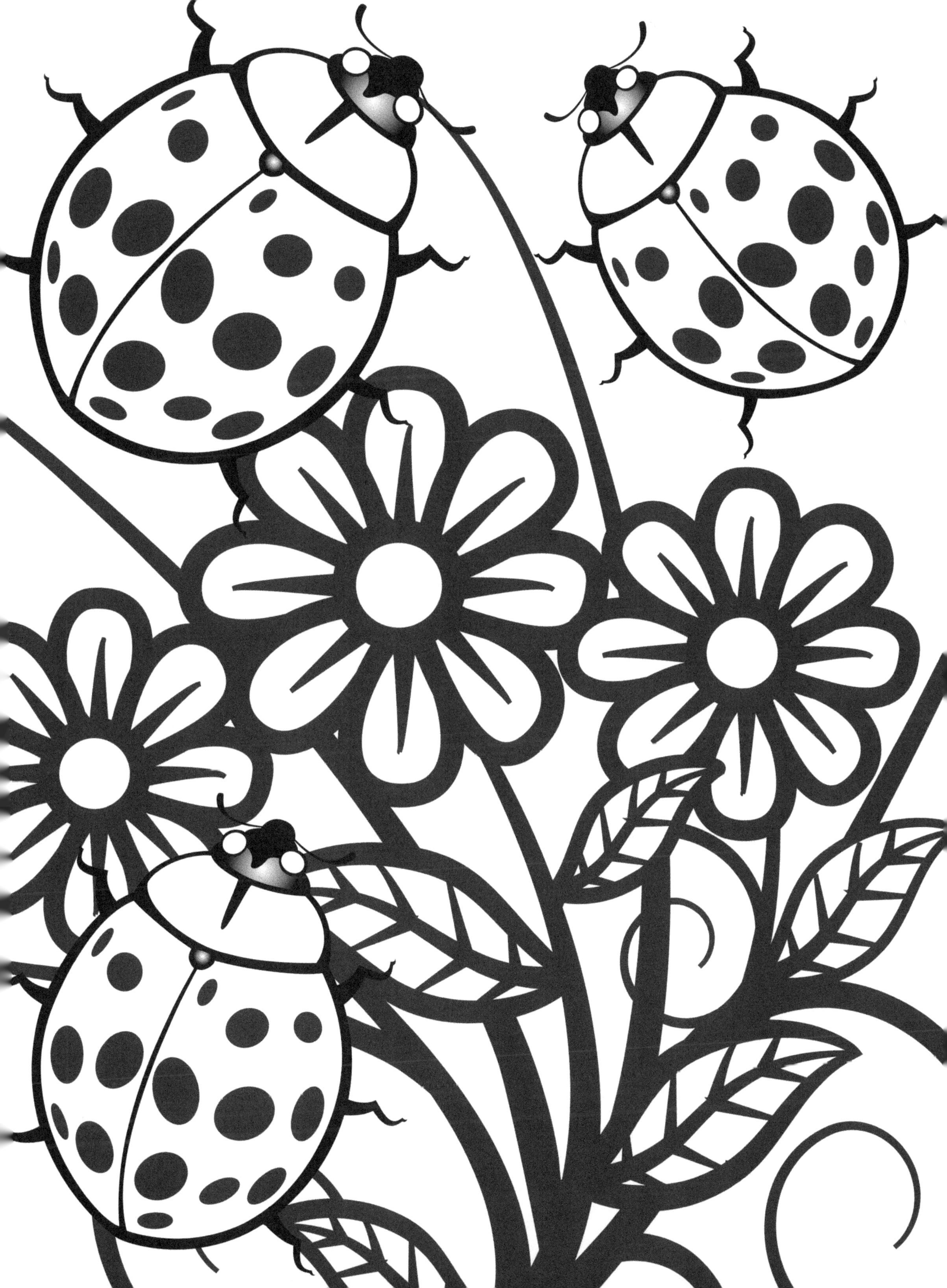

Blotter

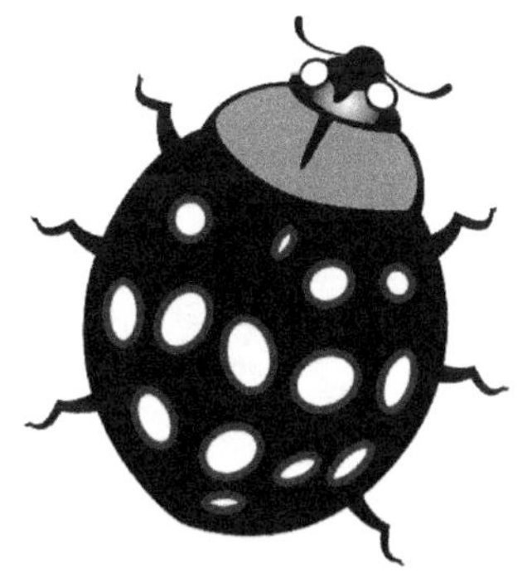

Blotter

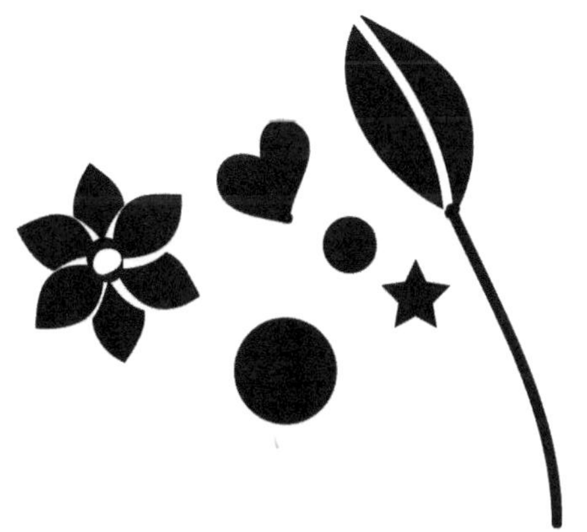

Show us what you love!
Pick your favorite page, color, and submit to unplugcoloring.com to receive exclusive bonus coloring pages!

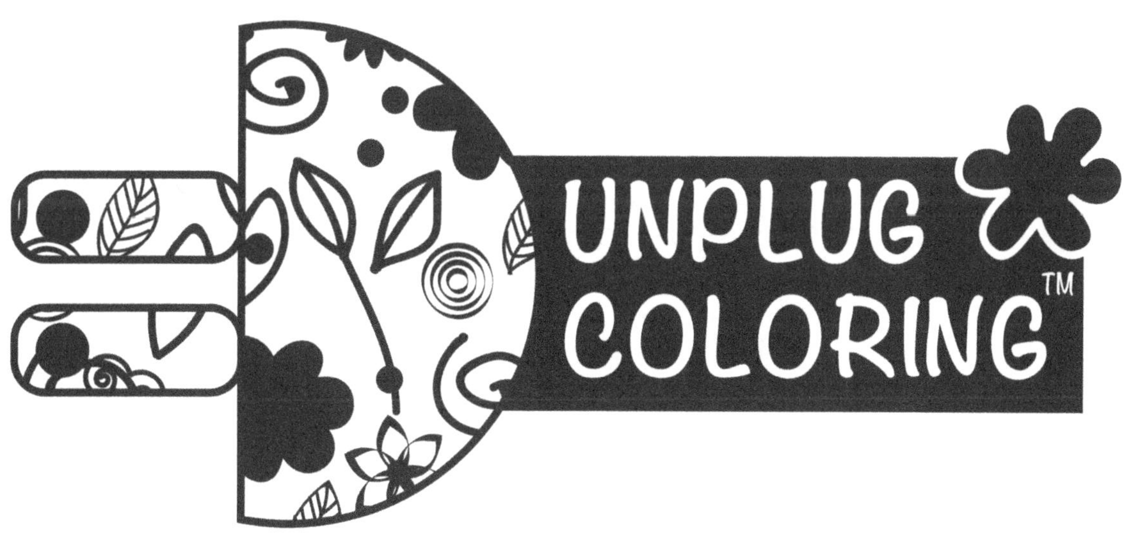

NATURE Unplug with ease... and Create is a perfect companion to the book
NATURE Unplug ... and Create
Share your coloring experience with friends and family!

Companion Edition also available from Unplug Coloring!

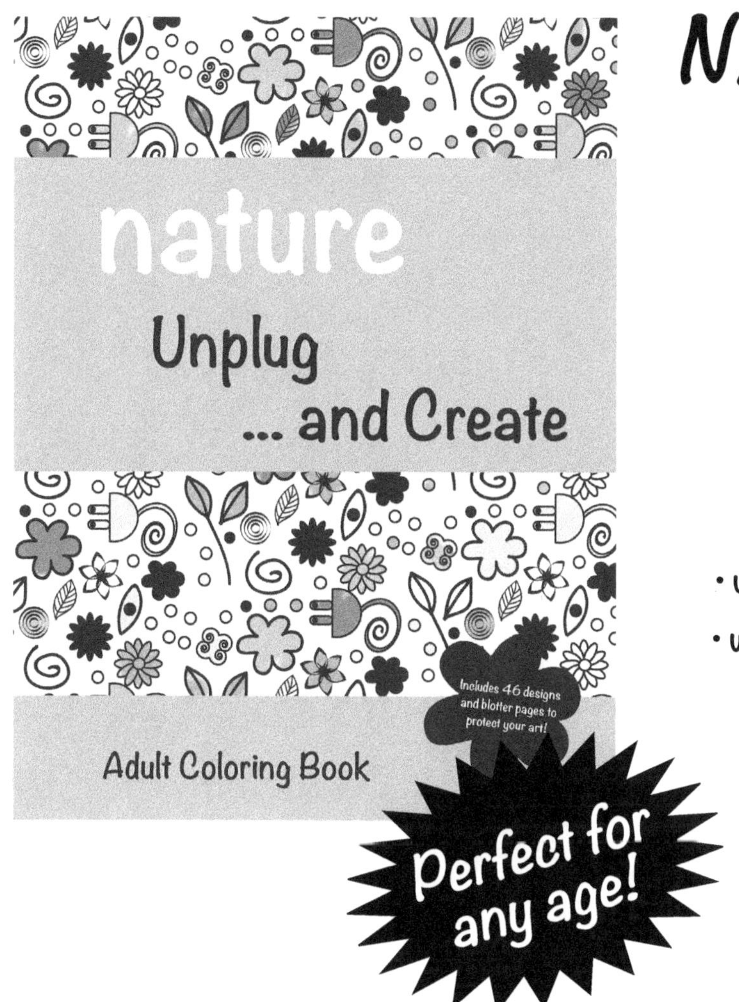

NATURE
Unplug
... and Create

Experience similar conceptual pages. This edition is geared to reconnect ...

- with your childhood and feel like a kid again
- with your calming and relaxing mental state
- with logical parts of the brain
- with yourself and combat anxiety
- and discover color to unwind
- and share with friends and family

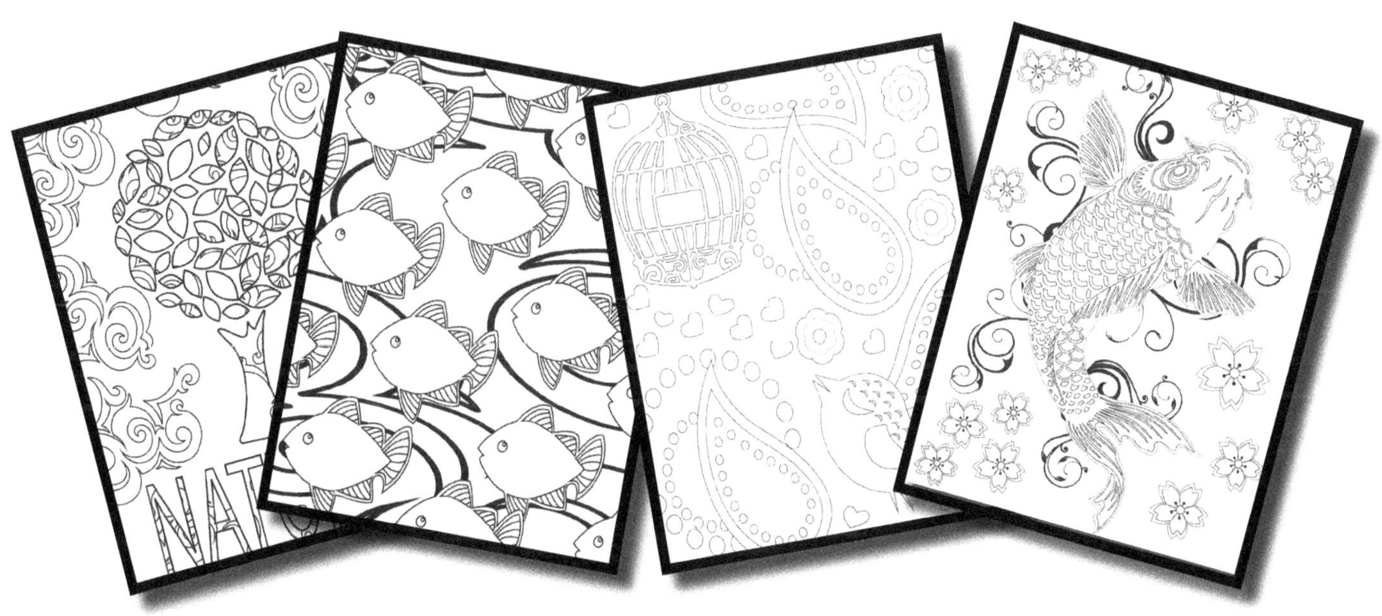

www.ingramcontent.com/pod-product-compliance
Lightning Source LLC
LaVergne TN
LVHW081403110826
845149LV00010B/1648
9780997490015